MODERN FASHION IN DETAIL

MODERN
FASHION
IN
DETAIL

BY CLAIRE WILCOX & VALERIE MENDES
PHOTOGRAPHY BY RICHARD DAVIS
LINE DRAWINGS BY LEONIE DAVIS

THE OVERLOOK PRESS
WOODSTOCK • NEW YORK

First published in 1991 by The Overlook Press,
Lewis Hollow Road, Woodstock, New York 12498
First paperback edition 1998

Library of Congress Cataloging-in-Publication Data

Wilcox, Claire
Modern fashion in detail/Claire Wilcox and Valerie Mendes.p.cm.

Costume design. I. Mendes, Valerie D. II. Title.author

TT507.W455 1992
746.9'2—dc20
91-28227 CIP
ISBN 0-87951-869-3

Designed by Area. Printed in China

With grateful thanks to everyone in the Textiles and Dress
Department especially Debbie Sinfield, Howard Batho and
Ngozi Ikoku; Lesley Burton and Jennifer Blain of the
Publications Section for their good advice and patience and to
Mark Wilcox and Julian Stair for their support.

Above all, we are indebted to the couturiers without whose
creative gifts this book would not have been possible.

Front cover: Detail of evening dress, knitted rayon jersey.
Yuki. London, late 1970s.

Back cover: Detail of evening dress, silk tulle,
jet with satin ribbon bows. Christian Dior.
French, Spring/Summer 1959.

CONTENTS

CRISTOBAL BALENCIAGA

PIERRE BALMAIN

PIERRE CARDIN

JOHN CAVANAGH

COCO CHANEL

SYBIL CONNOLLY

ANDRÉ COURRÈGES

CULTURE SHOCK

(YUZUN KOGA & JEANNIE MACARTHUR)

JEAN DESSÈS

CHRISTIAN DIOR

MATILDA ETCHES

MARIANO FORTUNY

MR FREEDOM

(TOMMY ROBERTS)

JOHN GALLIANO

BILL GIBB

HUBERT de GIVENCHY

MADAME GRÈS

KATHERINE HAMNETT

NORMAN HARTNELL

JACQUES HEIM

CHARLES JAMES

CHRISTIAN LACROIX

JEANNE LANVIN

LUCILE

(LADY DUFF GORDON)

EVA LUTYENS

MAINBOCHER

LUN-NA MENOH

(ATSUKO SHIMIZU)

DIGBY MORTON

JEAN MUIR
PABLO & DELIA
PAQUIN
PAUL POIRET
ANTONY PRICE
MARY QUANT
ZANDRA RHODES
YVES SAINT LAURENT
ELSA SCHIAPARELLI
VICTOR STEIBEL
EMANUEL UNGARO
PHILLIPE VENET
MADELEINE VIONNET
VIVIENNE WESTWOOD
CHARLES FREDERICK WORTH
YUKI

LIST OF DESIGNERS

Only a collection as
rich and varied as the Victoria and Albert
Museum's, containing works by the world's top fashion
designers, could inspire this unique celebration of their art and
craft. Histories of 20th century dress and monographs on
individual designers usually include a few details of fabric,
construction and trimming but this is the first time a whole
volume has been devoted entirely to close-ups illustrating in
detail the intricate skills of high fashion. Significant examples
of high style clothes, worn by a privileged few are here
brought into sharp focus, revealing why they are so special
and why they form a vital part of one of the
world's finest collections of decorative art.

Time is a critical factor.
Time to make these complex works, time to
wear them and time for both owner and onlookers to
enjoy them. It is evident that during the early years of the
century time was a more readily available commodity than it is
today. The ultra-fashionable woman of the early 1900s
followed custom by changing throughout the day from one
lavish outfit to another. Her clothes came from workrooms
where skilled seamstresses and embroideresses laboured many
hours in the construction and decoration of ornate concoctions
– skills still required in the ateliers of today's great

FOREWORD

VALERIE MENDES

embroidery and couture workshops (page 103*br*). However, the pace of urban existence has accelerated as the century has progressed and we now live in a world in which speed is master – in realms of travel, communication and production. 'Easy' and 'instant', watchwords of the late 20th century, pervade most aspects of daily life including the world of clothing. Dictated by practicalities and budget most women's wardrobes contain mass-produced or limited edition day clothes with perhaps one or two 'special occasion' dresses. On the whole, women buy ready-to-wear garments in which cost has necessarily limited the quality of finish and decoration; these goods meet the ravages of daily wear and tear and take their chances periodically in the washer and at the dry cleaners. As the illustrations reveal, dress collected by the Victoria and Albert Museum is far removed from such everyday attire.

Although heightened media awareness of stylish clothing has increased general interest in apparel we rarely have time or the opportunity to stop and study dress in minute detail. Delays while travelling by air, rail or road encourage idle contemplation of the contemporary, mainly off-the-peg look, but any closer inspection could be misunderstood. By contrast, it is enlightening to observe visitors to the Museum's dress display where the changing shape of clothes worn by our forebears attracts much comment. Visitors are intrigued by the minutiae of high fashion. Distanced from the objects by sheets of glass, they nevertheless spend many hours examining the components of each ensemble and remark about the time and skill it must have taken to achieve an ornately embroidered dress or a garment of particularly complex cut. Here we aim to extend that experience and bring readers into even closer contact with highlights from the collection.

Modern living has developed the throw-away ethos and customers are conditioned to purchase low cost clothes with an ephemeral life span. When a fashion has waned or a garment is past its best it is simply jettisoned. This suits the quick-turnover high street market fed by mass production in which, to ensure survival, the depth of every seam and every element of trimming is calculated, costed and minimised. 50 years ago (page 67) manufacturers were compelled by government 'Utility' edicts to make similar calculations, but then in an effort to save materials for the war effort, and not to make profits. In 1942, within tight constraints, a group of London-based designers succeeded in creating the classic 'Utility' collection that is still noteworthy for its streamlined elegance. This fact was recognised immediately by the Brooklyn Museum, New York which, with great foresight, tried to acquire the collection from the Board of Trade. Fortunately for the V&A, the Director of the Board, Sir Thomas Barlow, (originator of the Utility Fashion Designer venture) was most reluctant to see the results of his endeavours cross the Atlantic, so he quickly found a London home for them.

Attitudes to everyday wear have changed dramatically this century. Of necessity, during wartime the flow of fashion was interrupted and women had to 'make do and mend' in order to extend the useful life of their clothes. Ideas of clothes lasting and being repaired have now all but vanished and it is often the case that even slightly damaged garments are consigned to the rubbish bin or sent to charity and second hand outlets. In a different league, many clothes in this Museum were custom made by couturiers for important clients, and, though worn infrequently, were impeccably cared for, often by maids.

As special creations representing high points in design and construction they were treasured by their owners and eventually donated to the Museum to ensure their preservation. Sadly, though, it has to be admitted that before the fairly recent acknowledgement of dress as a major decorative art some important wardrobes were lost to posterity.

Each garment illustrated has many layers of significance which Claire Wilcox unravels in her revealing commentaries.

Clearly central to any analysis is the collection itself. Currently, two distinct strands contribute towards a clearly defined acquisition policy. First, clothes by leading couturiers in international cosmopolitan centres form the core of the collection and the focus of this book. These works exemplify peaks of achievement wherein a designer's vision has been realised in luxury fabrics by a skilled work force of seamstresses, tailors, embroiderers and finishers operating to the highest possible standards. Most of the images and interpretations in this volume offer the onlooker a reverse perspective through the couture procedure, travelling from a detail of the final work back through finishing, construction, cutting, calico toile, fabric choice and, where possible, to the designer's original concept.

To capture that shift in tradition which occurred in the 1960s the V&A also acquires clothes which, irrespective of standard of construction and finish, are deemed to be setting the 'alternative' fashionable pace. This forms the second strand of the Museum's acquisition policy. Thus a number of the details on these pages are taken from lively youth culture creations which are frequently linked to developments in popular music. In a cyclical manner these so-called street styles nowadays often inspire fashion's mainstream as illustrations in this book demonstrate.

Many clothes in the Museum collection had owners who were celebrities and known for their sophisticated or avant garde approach to dress (page 87). Other works are models which came straight from the designer's atelier having been worn just once at the seasonal fashion show. Sometimes we have been able to quote chapter and verse on where, when and how an outfit was worn thus adding a further social relevance to its history. Unearthing contemporary illustrations of garments in a newspaper, fashion magazine or society journal is always rewarding. For earlier 20th century objects it helps pin-point their dates and generally expands our understanding of the garments. Although the exact date of Zandra Rhodes' 'conceptual chic' evening sheath dress (page 111*bl*) is known, a poster of the pop singer Blondie (Debbie Harry) wearing an almost identical dress from the 'conceptual chic' collection (inspired by clothes worn by punks) adds a further dimension to the dress.

Close focus photographs have been taken specially by Richard Davis of the Museum's Photographic Studio. In many cases they are analogous to abstract works of art and occasionally it is difficult to imagine the whole garment from which they were extracted. To overcome this fact and illustrate the clothes in their entirety, each colour plate is accompanied by Leonie Davis's lucid and diagramatic line drawings which resemble those featured on the reverse of paper patterns. The photographs offer a unique chance to study the fabrics of fashion. Fashion designers have a punishing schedule dictated by the twice yearly couture and ready-to-wear shows, interspersed with mid-season collections as well as specialist ranges (sometimes under licence) including sportswear, childrenswear, accessories and extras such as perfumes and cosmetics. Choice of fabrics for each season is critical as it helps to define the parameters of the collection. Some couturiers are irrevocably associated with their favourite materials – thus Madeleine Vionnet and matt crepe are almost synonymous. Chanel was a devotee of soft woollen tweeds and Courrèges favoured densely woven worsteds. Also, certain fabrics can develop a symbolic relationship to the fashion trends of a particular period. Fluid crepe was ideal for Vionnet's body skimming bias cut dresses (page 125*tl*) just as textured tweeds were perfect for Chanel's classic suits (page 57) and Courrèges' revolutionary trouser suits and mini dresses of Spring 1964 had hard edges which could only be maintained by solid fabrics (page 23*br*). Sybil Connolly handled the light Irish linens in a masterly way (page 17) and few can match Jean Muir's dexterity with woollen crepe and jersey (page 23*bl*). The close ups show that throughout the century natural fabrics – fine silks, wools, cottons and linens have remained basic to high fashion though an adventurous spirit like Schiaparelli was not afraid of exploiting unconventional materials including coiled sprung wire (page 51*tl*). Almost fifty years later the irrepressible Vivienne Westwood employed the fabric used for making dishcloths with deliberate glee (page 81).

One of the aims of this book is to explore the appeal of the details of clothing conceived and executed by leaders in the field. The camera zooms onto a small section of each garment revealing elements which are essential to the success of high fashion. Thus we are invited to delight in the technically perfect seaming of a wedding dress designed by Charles James in 1934 (page 19) or admire the precision necessary to achieve the faultlessly quilted geometric hem of a 1960s mini-dress by Pierre Cardin (page 125*bl*). Balenciaga excelled in the art of garment finishing – the insides of garments bearing his label are as perfect as the outsides – hems, seams, buttonholes and linings are impeccable. So pure is the cut of day wear by Balenciaga that it proved impossible to capture in close up. We elected to represent his major contribution to 20th century fashion by an extrovert evening design where, with undeniable skill, he engineered button holes in deeply encrusted embroidered silk (page 131). The Victoria and Albert's collection of work by Yves Saint Laurent is not extensive but includes significant pieces such as a lavishly embroidered mini-dress which inventively shades from white paillettes to a dense, black, ostrich feather hem (page 103*br*).

The illustrations highlight a vital area of the fashion business that is often overlooked – the trimmings industry. Traditionally the manufacture or import of items such as buttons, beads, sequins, fastenings, belts, buckles and fashion findings has been undertaken by small scale, specialised companies. All western urban centres have such establishments and none more so than Paris. International democratisation of fashion and production of cheap, easy to buy, ready-to-wear clothes combined with the reduction of home and professional dressmaking has meant a dramatic decline in these once thriving enterprises. Haberdashery and trimming catalogues dating from before World War II confirm the riches then available and point up the paucity of the mass-produced, bubble packed trimmings on sale now. Total mass-produced uniformity will be avoided as long as top fashion designers continue to require highly individualised trimmings and commission unique pieces from the surviving specialists. Many of the larger couture houses once had their own embroidery workrooms but with fashion changes in the second half of the 20th century these were cut back and many were closed. Fortunately the demands of high fashion have meant that the great embroidery houses such as Lesage continue to flourish.

Chapters in this book
are organised thematically and there is
no attempt to chart any chronological evolution of detail in fashion. Many elements link each chapter but perhaps the most obvious connection is designer wit made manifest in cloth, trimmings and fastenings. Even the most serious of couturiers have been known to incorporate amusing touches in their designs. It is a truism that fashion (even high fashion) and fun are partners. Buttons and bows lend themselves to frivolity and variations are infinite from Schiaparelli's energetic metal acrobats (page 75) to Bill Gibb's whimsical insignia bees (page 77) and Vivienne Westwood's idiosyncratic Vim lids

(page 81). Christian Lacroix brings to his work a highly advanced sense of humour combined with a museum-like knowledge of historical dress. Best known for mixing different vibrantly patterned and coloured fabrics here we show a Lacriox bow in subdued black juxtaposed with stripes and polka dots printed on an alarming fluorescent green (page 91tr). Large bows are not the most practical of decorative devices but lend romantic and lighthearted notes often to the back of fashionable dress. In his ultra-feminine designs Christian Dior made masterly use of bows of all types and dimensions and after his death his house continued the tradition (page 87). Pleats can be manipulated to suggest winged creatures or flight which Anthony Price imaginatively captured in an assymetrical pure white sheath dress (page 39). Even the tailored basics of inset pockets, seams and fly front fastening are treated to Culture Shock's witty puns (page 51tr). Embroidery studding and appliqué can be used in free manner much like an artist uses paints. Mr Freedom amused all comers to his lively boutique with visual jokes including his painter's smock (page 51br), while more recently, Katherine Hamnett elevates a biker jacket to higher realms and adds an amusing monogrammed heart (page 129).

This compilation gives
us an opportunity to focus on details of
some of the more practical aspects and some of the hidden delights of high fashion which are often overlooked
in more conventional explorations
of the subject.

SEAMS

CORDED seams form a
series of bold, vertical contour lines on this moss
green, Irish linen dress. The firm cording is covered with
smooth, bias cut linen giving it a precise linear quality. These
seams are both decorative and structural, providing a textural
contrast to the softly irregular and horizontal pleating
of the panels which they join together to
make up the dress.

Sybil Connolly employs a fresh approach to a
familiar dressmaking device to suit her clean, uncluttered
approach to design. The cording emphasises the feminine
shape of this classic princess line dress, which is of
12 shaped panels. Short, cap sleeves are cut in one with the
dress, and have small, diamond shaped underarm gussets to
allow ease of movement and comfort. Matching cuffs are
attached bias strips of fabric tied in knots at the
upper arms. Echoing the corded seams the wide neck is edged
with covered cord, which continues around the low,
V-shaped back.

The designer opened one of the first couture houses
in Ireland and is famed for her use of indigenous Irish textiles
such as linens and tweeds, and for her use of subtle, natural
colours. *Vogue* illustrated a similar dress to that shown here in
March 1957; 'The look is linen – wonderful Irish linen – a
myriad of tiny, tiny pleats. Yet crumple it into a suitcase and it
will emerge, uncrushed, uncrushable, to sweep grandly
through a season of gaiety'.

Irish handkerchief linen day
dress with self-covered corded seams
Sybil Connolly. Irish, 1955-7
Label: Sybil Connolly Dublin classics
Given by Mrs V Laski
T.174 & A-1973

CHARLES James said 'all my seams have meaning – they emphasise something about the body' [1]. This wedding dress of 1934, an early example of the designer's work, has seams that contour the smooth ivory satin to cling to and drape from the svelte body. While being very much of its time, the dress also foreshadows later developments in the designer's oeuvre, particularly his approach to complex cut in his avowed intention to celebrate the female figure.

The back bodice drops in a V-line to the waist and is cut in one with the sleeves. Five small darts fit the main dress into the base of the yoke, as shown, and the bust darts go around the side, shaping the area over the hips, almost to the centre back seam. Other details include underarm gussets, darts at the elbow and fitted cuffs with faced points and press stud fastening. The high neck has small folds at the front and fastens at the back with a hook and loop. In traditional manner it was trimmed with orange blossom. The skirt is cut on the bias with a dipping flounce at the front trailing into a divided train terminating in two points.

The beauty of the dress lies in its deceptive simplicity, and the designer's complete understanding of the potential of the material. Simple details of darts and seams become abstracted into a formal pattern while serving to delineate and enhance the grace of the figure. James said that fashion is 'what is rare, correctly proportioned and, though utterly discreet, libidinous' [2].

Wedding dress, silk satin with orange blossom trimming. Charles James. English, 1934. Worn by Miss 'Baba' Beaton on her marriage to Mr Alec Hambro, 6 November 1934, and given by Mrs Alec Hambro T.271 & A-1974

1. *The Genius of Charles James,* The Brooklyn Museum, New York, 1982, p. 84.
2. *Ibid* p. 84.

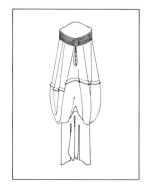

ZANDRA Rhodes utilises
the plain seam by simply reversing it so
that the edges become a decorative feature in this bright blue
chiffon evening dress. A horizontal seam, set half-way down
the draped outer skirt, runs the entire circumference of the
dress. Its edges are hand rolled and trimmed with a double row
of miniscule gold beads which draw attention to the inside-
out seam and also weight the fine, translucent chiffon, assisting
the drapes and folds of the light, floating fabric. The gilded,
round beads echo the bright, gold pigment of the printed
pattern. The linear, swirling printed design of stylised faces,
with its painterly vitality, is typical of Zandra Rhodes' surface
decoration and is an ideal complement to the
ethereal, intensely blue chiffon.

The dress has a strapless
yoke top in gold satin, topstitched
and embellished with gold stars, beads and paste and an
overskirt with a rolled and beaded hem. It drapes at the front
to reveal an underskirt of blue silk with floating panels,
weighted on three sides with additional gold beads. Mariano
Fortuny weighted the hems and sleeves of his pleated silk
Delphos gowns with Venetian glass beads in the early part of
this century but Zandra Rhodes reworks this practical and
decorative idea with her own characteristic
style and verve.

Evening dress, printed
silk chiffon, silk, sequins, beads, paste stones
Worn with a pleated cap in blue satin.
Zandra Rhodes. English, 1979. Given by Miss Zandra Rhodes
Label: Zandra Rhodes Sample
T. 283-1980

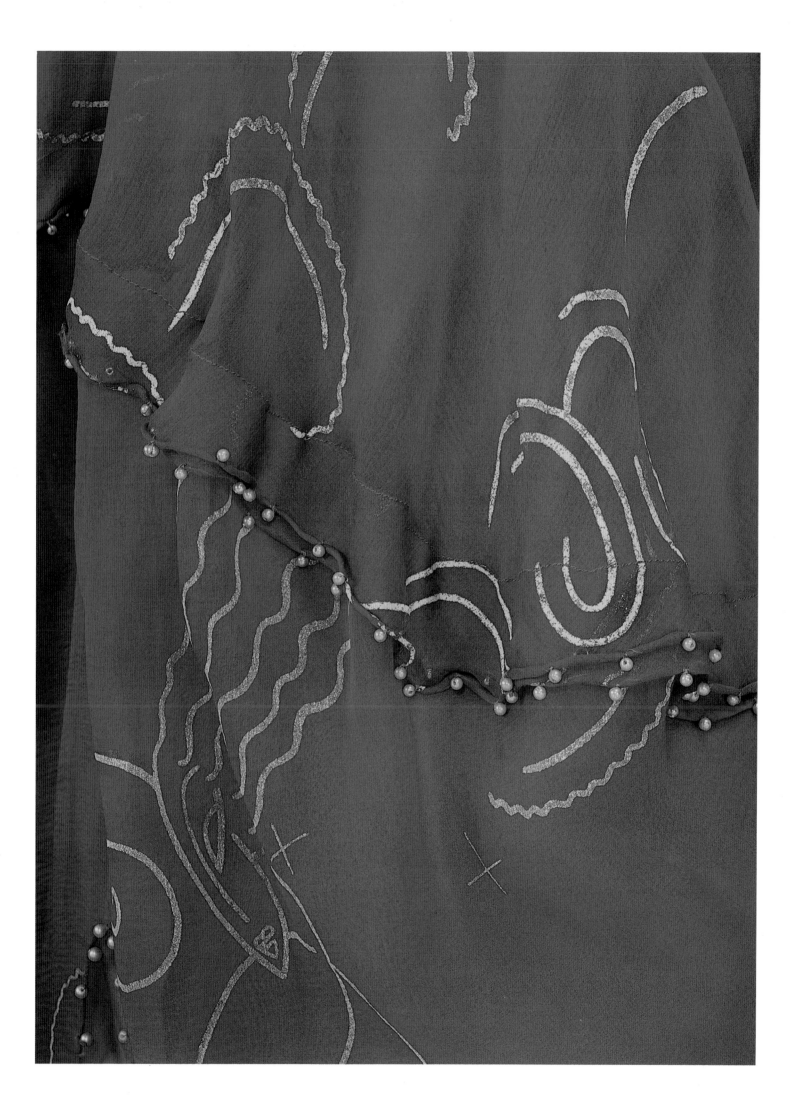

A BIAS cut, inset panel
on the back of this tailored jacket in a
woven brown and white check wool provides a variation of
pattern, emphasised by the curved, topstitched seams which
run from shoulder to hem.

Immaculately tailored, this outfit employs traditional
construction techniques and clever seaming with
great economy and style.

Jacket and skirt, woven wool
Probably John Cavanagh. English, Autumn 1942
Label: a small luggage label inscribed 'No 20 Original C92/10'
(the maximum selling price of just under £5 or $8.50)
Given by the Board of Trade
T.48 & A-1942

MOST of the decorative
and seamed detail is concentrated on
the bodice of this scarlet rayon crepe day dress of 1942,
designed under the war-time Utility Scheme. Yoke and collar
are cut in one with the narrow outer side panels. The yoke's
edge is faced and stitched onto the lower bodice in scalloped
seams. Narrow inverted pleats with a double row of
topstitching in thick, shiny scarlet rayon thread run vertically
either side of the centre front which fastens with self covered
buttons and neatly bound buttonholes.

Day dress, matt rayon
crepe with topstitching in rayon thread
Probably Victor Steibel. English, Autumn 1942
Utility Original Model No 23, maximum retail selling price
53/7 (£2.68p or $4.50 approx). Given by
the Board of Trade
T.58 & A-1942

JEAN Muir's jersey
dress in cobalt blue exemplifies all the
precision and detail that this designer is renowned for.
Decorative machine topstitching on the long cuffs follows the
outline of the curved corners to fill the cuff entirely. This
immaculate topstitching gives body to the soft, light material
and crisp edges to the closely fitting cuffs and similarly treated
collar on an otherwise loose and fluid garment. Sleeves are set
in with topstitched box pleats and tucks, and the shoulders are
lightly padded. The steep yoke is joined to the main dress with
topstitched welt seams from which the flaring, unlined skirt
falls. Of complex cut it consists of 20 narrow fabric panels which
utilise the flowing, draping qualities of the fabric.

Day dress, matt viscose jersey
Jean Muir. English, 1974. Label: Jean Muir London
Given by Celestine Dars
T.143-1985

THE crisply tailored look
of this double breasted, mini-length coat of
1967 is typical of Courrèges' structured, linear style, and of his
concentration on fine finish and detail. Attention is
deliberately drawn to the visible construction lines of the
garment. The photograph focuses on just one false pocket flap,
an inset side panel and a button and illustrates the confident,
white machine topstitching and welt seam which emphasise
the cut and shaping of the garment.
The pliable weightiness
of the woven gaberdine fabric is perfectly matched to the
almost architectural qualities of Courrèges' styling.

Coat, woven woollen gaberdine
André Courrèges. French, Winter 1967
Label: Courrèges Paris. Worn by the late Mrs Stavros Niarchos
and given by Mr Stavros Niarchos
T.102-1974

AN EVOCATIVE
summer dress dating from early this century is
entirely hand made in frail lace, crocheted flowers and white
cotton lawn. The detail shows the extensive use of insertion
lace and crochet to create an apparently seamless skirt,
although in fact it consists of a multitude of virtually invisible,
hand-stitched joins. The technique of insertion suits the open
nature of lace and crochet. Here the lawn fabric base is
carefully trimmed away and is almost entirely replaced by a
patchwork of zig-zag sections which achieve a light and
delicate look. The shape of the flared, trained skirt is
determined by wide inset godets, echoed by bands of crochet
and rows of tiny, handstitched pin-tucks. Within a unifying
all-white scheme a wealth of tiny floral patterns of varying
scale and contrasting texture satisfied the early 1900s fashion
for costly detail. The modishly bloused bodice is adorned with
larger clusters of hand crocheted flowers, its V-neck edged
with a gathered net frill while its elbow length sleeves are
minutely pin-tucked and lace edged. The back fastens with tiny
mother-of-pearl buttons and handworked loops.

The Lady's Realm in 1907 remarked that; 'July is
the ideal month in England where dress is concerned, and our
thoughts turn to transparent lawns, ethereal muslins and
dainty laces which are all associated with the summer
confections of London and Paris'[1]. Soft and pliable, these
dresses were underpinned by rigid corseting beneath the
frothy lace and lawn.

Day dress,
cotton lawn, lace and cotton
hand crochet. French(?), 1904-8
Given by The Baron Charles de Menasce
T.107-1939

1. Vol. XXII, p. 24

24

GATHERS, TUCKS
& PLEATS

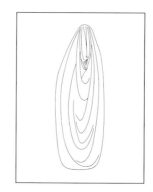

THE rich, rose pink
jersey fabric of this sleeveless evening dress
drapes and flows in soft gathers around the body, supported
solely by the simple halter neck. The supple material falls
dramatically from a single point at the front where the
concentration of gathers is caught neatly with a few stitches.
The minimal construction and seaming on this nevertheless
complex dress relies on the light and fluid knitted fabric taking
its form and structure from the body beneath. Falling in pliant
folds to the ground, where it drapes either side of the feet, the
dress extends at the back to become a hooded cloak. Off the
body, the garment resembles a limp almost shapeless length of
luxurious fabric, but once on, it is animated and made
comprehensible by the figure underneath.

The theatrical cut,
clinging sensual fabric and rich colour of
Yuki's draped evening gowns demand wearers with great
confidence and style.

Evening dress, knitted rayon jersey
Yuki. London, late 1970s. Label: None
Worn and given by Gayle Hunnicutt
T.263-1989

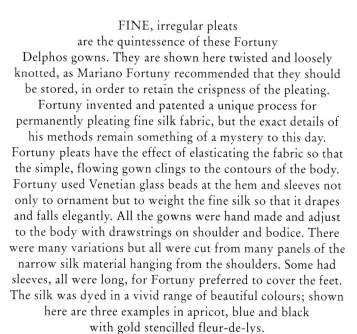

FINE, irregular pleats
are the quintessence of these Fortuny
Delphos gowns. They are shown here twisted and loosely
knotted, as Mariano Fortuny recommended that they should
be stored, in order to retain the crispness of the pleating.
Fortuny invented and patented a unique process for
permanently pleating fine silk fabric, but the exact details of
his methods remain something of a mystery to this day.
Fortuny pleats have the effect of elasticating the fabric so that
the simple, flowing gown clings to the contours of the body.
Fortuny used Venetian glass beads at the hem and sleeves not
only to ornament but to weight the fine silk so that it drapes
and falls elegantly. All the gowns were hand made and adjust
to the body with drawstrings on shoulder and bodice. There
were many variations but all were cut from many panels of the
narrow silk material hanging from the shoulders. Some had
sleeves, all were long, for Fortuny preferred to cover the feet.
The silk was dyed in a vivid range of beautiful colours; shown
here are three examples in apricot, blue and black
with gold stencilled fleur-de-lys.

Fortuny gowns were
influenced by the late 19th century dress
reform movement, and were initially worn by dancers and
actresses such as Isadora Duncan and Sarah Bernhardt. Others
began to wear them as informal tea gowns but later they
became more acceptable for evening wear outside the home. In
a letter dated 25th June 1923 the sculptor Hamo Thorneycroft
described his daughter in a pure white Delphos which she gave
the Museum in 1982, '...Elfrida...looking lovely in her silk
Greek clinging dress – white, against the light of the Jap
lanterns outside...'[1]. These romantic robes, inspired by Greek
draped statuary, captivated many people; Lady Diana Cooper
wrote of the 'timeless dresses of pure thin silk severely cut
straight from shoulder to toe and kept wrung like skein of
wool. In every crude and subtle colour, they clung like a
mermaid's scales'[2].

Delphos robes, pleated silk, with Venetian glass beads.
Mariano Fortuny. Italian, c.1909-20
T. 731 & A-1972 (black and gold), given by Elizabeth Sweeting
on behalf of the late Fr. Sebastian Bullough, worn by the
actress Eleanora Duse
T.174-1967 (blue), worn by Miss Emilie Grigsby
T.193 & A-1974 (apricot), given by Miss Irene Worth

1. *The Rainbow Comes
and Goes*, London, 1958, Lady Diana Cooper, p. 61.
2. Elfrida Manning, *Marble and Bronze. The Art and Life of Hamo
Thorneycroft*, Trefoil Books, London, 1982, p. 185.

ROSES gathered from
folds of ivory silk fabric cluster and
trail over the shoulder and back of this wedding coat by John
Galliano. The garland starts with small buds, gradually
growing to full soft blooms. More roses, made from satin and
chiffon with organza leaves, are placed amongst the
complex folds of material.

The coat is cut with fabric
extensions, providing flaps which Galliano catches and
rolls together to form these decorative flourishes. The folding
also serves to shape the garment in the manner of more
conventional fabric gathers. Fastening with a single concealed
button, the coat has long sleeves with dropped shoulders and a
low waist seam. The skirt back is elaborately draped with
curved front edges. It was worn over a matching, strapless
dress with shirred sides and roses at the hips. The small
bridesmaids were dressed in simple, front buttoning, white
dresses with cross-over skirts each decorated
with a single rose.

Fabric flowers are not new but these are unusual, forming an
integral part of the garment as if grown from the fabric itself.
The delicate shades of ivory and white silk, tumbling roses and
romantic styling make a unique wedding outfit.

Wedding outfit, silk,
with satin, chiffon and organza fabric flowers
John Galliano. English, Summer 1987
Label: John Galliano London Made in Britain
Worn and given by Francesca Oddi
T.41 to E-1988

CRISP accordion pleats
transform the silk grosgrain fabric of
this unusual, short evening cape, allowing it to swing and
ripple with every movement. The ingenious construction of
this over garment, which Matilda Etches patented in 1953,
forms a double-layered, all-in-one cape that swings in a
continuous movement around the shoulders and falls in two
layers of stiff folds at the back, the outer flared, the inner
straight. A flattering, high stand collar encircles
the neck, dipping at the rear.

The fabric is constructed of numerous strips
of 'ribbon', seamed vertically and pleated afterwards. These
vertical pleats are further emphasised by the strongly defined
silk stripes in red, maroon, and black, edged with plain bands.
Matilda Etches used a form of permanent pleating which is not
concerned with soft, fluid movement but which imbues the
fabric with a rigid, sculptural quality. The light silk acquires an
elasticated flexibility across its width enabling it to enfold the
shoulders and torso and to hang in stiff, straight pleats from
neck to serrated hem. This is a garment in which function gives
way to remarkable and innovative construction and
purely decorative impact.

Evening cape, silk 'ribboning'
Matilda Etches. USA, 1949
Label: Matilda Etches Patent Pending
Given by Mrs Matilda Etches-Homan
T.185-1969

FINE, regular pleating of
this graceful, white, silk jersey dress
creates a gown of statuesque lines. In a fluid diagonal
movement, the wide, single shoulder strap crosses and
supports the bodice, leaving the other shoulder bare.

The fine silk jersey is
given density and substance by the pleats
slip-stitched onto white organza, over a foundation of firmly
boned bodice with underwired bust. Bodice and skirt are made
together from vertically joined lengths of silk, simply
topstitched to form the waist from which the long,
columnar skirt falls.

Evening dress, silk jersey with tie belt
Madame Grès. French, 1968. Label: Gres 1 Rue de la Paix
Worn and given by Princess Stanislaus Radziwill
T.250 & A-1974

HUNDREDS of tiny pin-tucks
cover the entire surface of both dress and
coat in this blue-green silk ensemble by Hartnell.
The curved yoke of the coat is formed from interwoven strips
of silk in a simple basket weave, a play upon the construction
of woven fabric which is further emphasised by the patterning
of the narrow tucks. The wide, elbow length sleeves and the
short, unfitted coat flare by means of gradually widening,
vertical tucks which enhance the full cut. In contrast,
the sleeveless, V-necked dress is fitted with a
darted, pin-tucked bodice and straight skirt
constructed from interwoven strips.

Day outfit, dress and coat, silk taffeta
Norman Hartnell. English, 1958
Label: Hartnell London Paris
Given and worn by Mrs Wyndgate
T.170 & A-1990

THE overlapping,
curved pleats formed into scalloped panels
on this bodice front suggest a stylised rendition of receding
waves, an impression further enhanced by the deep sea-blue of
the fine, slightly stiff, silk fabric. The controlled movement on
the curved, fitted bodice is achieved by the dexterous pleating
of fabric cut on the cross, fronted with no visible seams.

The scalloped pleating
encloses the front torso up to the low,
strapless décolletage, and continues across the back in straight,
horizontal lines. The bodice fits the figure tightly to the hips
and from there the skirt falls in long, soft pleats.

Cocktail ensemble, silk Jean Dessès.
French, 1950s. Label: Jean Dessès 17 Avenue Matignon Paris
Worn and given by HRH Princess Margaret
T.237 & A-1986

THIS summer day
dress in duck egg blue silk crepe is
ornamented with panels of narrow pin-tucks, hand stitched in
matching thread. These gather the bodice at the shoulders and
waist with semi-pressed, narrow pleats. The low waist seam is
curved to a point at the centre front from which the calf-length
skirt falls, initially in a curved panel of pin-tucking, then in
narrow pleats which reach to the hem. The tucks serve to both
decorate and structure the fine, soft, unlined dress.
The tucks provide a linear,
vertical patterning which enhances
the straight lines of the dress. This is further echoed by
geometric, drawn threadwork on the bodice front, short
sleeves and long streamers which tie in a bow at the collar.

Summer day dress, silk crepe. Possibly Lanvin
French, c.1928. Worn by Miss Emilie Grigsby
T.141-1967

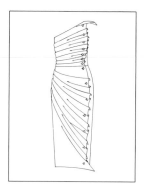 

CLOSELY swathing the
figure, the silk taffeta of this dramatically
structured garment is formed into large, irregular gathers
diagonally positioned across the front. These culminate in an
asymmetrical bodice, with an extraordinary, gravity defying
shoulder extension. Antony Price called this his 'Bird's Wing'
dress; the rigid folds of fabric with their feathered and
serrated edge evoke associations of flight
and movement.

The simple, white taffeta,
with its glossy, reflective sheen
offsets the complex structure of the garment. His choice of a
stiff fabric allows the raised folds to retain their shape and
make the dress virtually self-supporting. The folds are held in
place by large, self-covered buttons which secure the dress at
the side, and also provide an important visual motif. In
contrast the back is quite plain, a simple bodice with a single
shoulder strap and a straight, skirt fitted with darts
into the waist seam.

The bizarre and elegant
gown seems to enfold the body in an
articulated casing; its morphological associations prompting its
inclusion in the recent London showing at the V&A of the
exhibition from the Fashion Institute of Technology, New
York, called *Fashion and Surrealism*.

Evening dress, silk taffeta
Antony Price. English, Winter 1986. Label: None
Given by Antony Price
T.345-1989

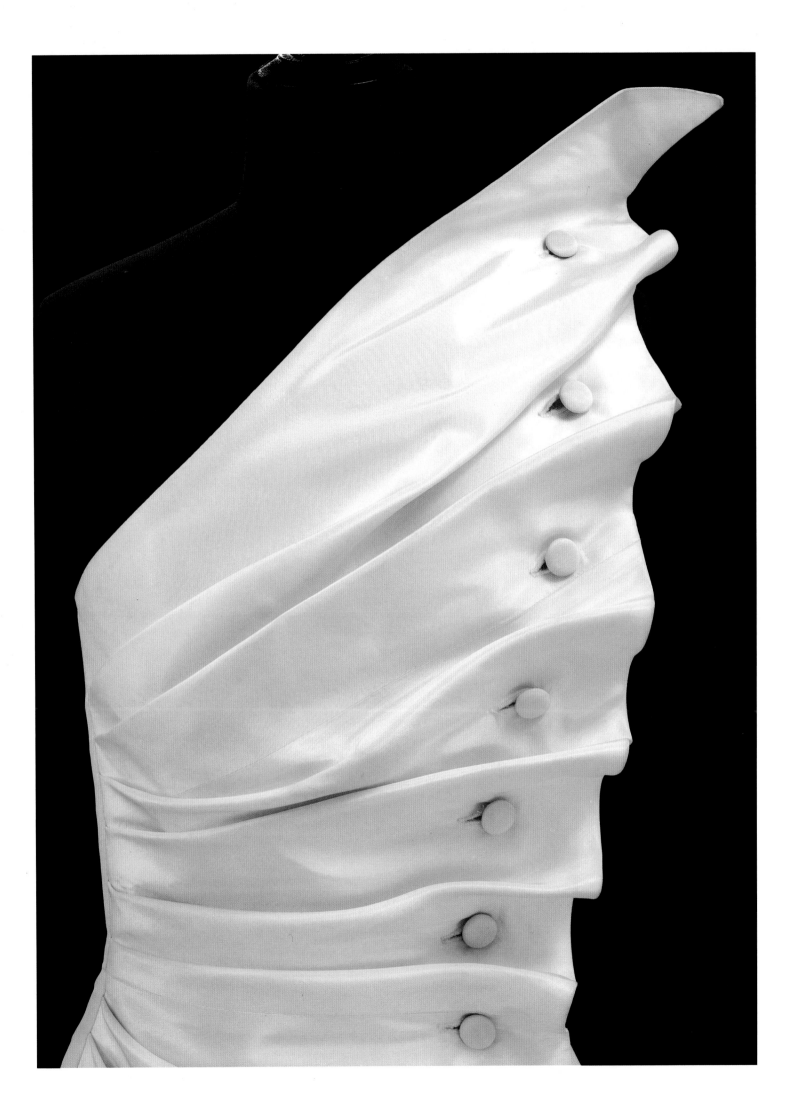

HAND ruching creates a
densely textured surface on this short
evening cape of deep purple silk velvet. The tight gathers of the
fabric concentrate large amounts of material into a small area
giving the cape substance and weight. The depth of the
irregular folds produces tones of light and shade within the
single colour of the velvet. A variation in pattern is also
created by directional changes of the ruching on the
component panels which form the cape. The wide, very deep
collar and flared, lower cape are ruched horizontally, while the
yoke and fitted shoulder area beneath the collar are ruched
vertically. The velvet is worked onto a silk voile foundation
and the cape is lined with purple satin, matching the
accompanying evening dress. The cape fastens with large,
domed, silvered glass buttons.

Lanvin uses a simple
technique to imbue the fabric of this
cape with a luxurious intensity of texture matched by the
rich colour. The fabric also acquires a heavy, moulded
quality which contrasts with the svelte, body hugging
satin dress beneath.

Evening cape, velvet and dress, satin
Jeanne Lanvin. French, 1935
Label: Jeanne Lanvin, Paris, unis France, Hiver 1935
Given by Miss I L Martin and worn
by Mrs L E Poulter
T.340 & A-1965

KNIFE-PLEATED gold
and silver lamé is wrought into swirls
which form the elevated 'sleeves' of this fantastic outfit by
Zandra Rhodes. The designer uses a modern, synthetic fabric
to conjure up the splendours of an earlier epoch of fashion.
Lamé is given a flexibility by the pleating which allows an
extraordinary fluid effect. Swirls resembling large, exotic
shells sit poised on the shoulders, and the light, metallic lamé
appears bright and airy against the black of the
quilted, laced, satin bodice.

A knife-pleated
overskirt of black tulle, screen printed with
Zandra Rhodes' 'Mexican Fan' pattern lies over a similarly
pleated underskirt of gold lamé, which glistens from beneath.
Extravagant overpanniers are balanced on the hips echoing the
opulent sleeves and are supported by boned calico
underpanniers. Before completing her 'Elizabethan Collection'
of 1981, from which this rich, fantasy ensemble is taken,
Zandra Rhodes studied historical precedents of 18th century
court wear in the Victoria and Albert Museum's
Dress Collection.

Evening ensemble 'Renaissance, Cloth of Gold Crinoline',
bodice, skirt, and overskirt over hoops, in satin, silk net, and
polyamide, polyester and metal lamé. Zandra Rhodes
English, Autumn/Winter 1981
Label: A Zandra Rhodes Sample
Given by Miss Zandra Rhodes
T.124 to C-1983

COLLARS, CUFFS
& POCKETS

THE high collar of Lanvin's
ingeniously cut satin evening jacket crosses
smoothly over to fasten with a spherical, ridged brass button
through a neatly made, bound buttonhole. Two lines of
topstitching run diagonally from shoulder seams to front
edges, giving the collar the appearance of being a separate piece
seamed to the fronts – however, it is cleverly cut in one with
the garment's front panels.

Inspired by the
flat planes of traditional Japanese attire the
jacket's Far Eastern look is reinforced by kimono sleeves
which are cut in one with the fronts of the jacket and the
shoulder seams left open to reveal, seductively, the upper arms.
Shaped panels are inset at the sides from cuff to hem, allowing
freedom of movement. The jacket wraps over asymmetrically
to fasten at the waistline with a second brass button above
the triangular, cut away front.

Parallel rows of narrow,
machine topstitching cover the entire
garment, emphasising its linear cut. The precise diagonal lines
at the front and emphatic horizontal lines across the back
finely quilt the citron coloured satin. Lanvin's inventive
manipulation of fabric creates a stylish yet warm jacket for
cold evenings. The jacket was originally part of an evening
ensemble but unfortunately the rest of the outfit has not
survived. Showing minute attention to detail, the buttons with
their ridged decoration were obviously carefully selected to
echo the garment's lines of topstitching.

Evening jacket, machine stitched satin
Jeanne Lanvin. French, Winter 1936-37
Label: Hiver 1936-1937 Jeanne Lanvin Paris, France. 15 7
Worn and given by Mrs John Guinness
T.223-1976

CREAMY white, fine
woollen cloth is exquisitely moulded by
rows of topstitched pleats from elbow to cuff on this full and
lavish sleeve. The pleats release into soft full folds at the outer
arm, forming decorative puffs of fabric while each cuff is
encircled with cream velvet ribbon which gathers the edging
of delicate lace. Tops of the elaborate three-quarter length
'leg of mutton' sleeves are gathered into the yoke and are
decorated, like the bodice and lower skirt, with a roundel
design of closely spaced cutwork which is edged with
fine cream silk cord.

The bodice has a high
standing collar and V-shaped chemisette,
with crochet trim. The side fronts are gathered into the yoke
and waist giving a highly fashionable pouched effect reinforced
by ornate trimming of lace and velvet ribbon swags. The skirt
consists of four panels tightly gathered into the broad, curved
waistband which is broken at the front and trimmed
at the back with velvet ribbon.

This refined day
gown of 1903-5 was probably made for spring-
time wear when the warm wool would protect against chilly
weather. Woollen face cloth was a fashionable material during
this period and the richly detailed dress, worked with its white
on white colour scheme, forms a harmonious composition,
featuring the elaborate sleeves and cuffs.

Day gown,
woollen face cloth, velvet and lace
English or French, 1903-5
Given by Lady Hoyer Miller
Circ. 175-1961

TIGHTLY coiled, overlapping
metal springs cover the pocket flaps and collar on this evening
jacket by Schiaparelli.

A garment which caused astonishment at the
time of its design, the jacket now seems feminine and
harmoniously composed. Here Schiaparelli does not
experiment with cut or construction; the shape remains that of
the classic 1930s silhouette. Schiaparelli was a great decorator
and innovator, alternating between the
bizarre and the lyrical.

Evening jacket, woollen cloth.
Elsa Schiaparelli. London c.1936-8
Label: Schiaparelli London
Worn and given by Lady Glenconner
T.63-1967

FOUR slanted, welt pockets are
features on this offbeat jacket with its bespoke 'tailoring'
theme. Large, hand tucked stitches are worked in
white thread, and a narrow, black and white 'tape
measure' trims the front edge.

The garment was among 21 customised Levi
denim jackets commissioned in aid of the Prince's Trust by
Blitz magazine in 1986. The famous detailing of Levi Strauss
denims is reworked; denim forms the shirt collar and V-
shaped, back insets while the flat seaming on the jacket back
copies the traditional Levi's construction.

Jacket, woven woollen cloth, denim
Culture Shock (Yuzun Koga and Jeannie Macarthur)
English, Summer 1986. Label: Culture Shock
T.149-1986

THE meticulously detailed
pocket flaps on this tailor-made day outfit in
charcoal grey wool and mohair are totally decorative – there
are no pockets. The large flaps are set into the raised waistline
and are piped at the edges in black velvet printed with narrow,
cross hatched, pale grey stripes. Each pocket has two pairs of
bold 'fastenings', large velvet covered buttons joined by
decorative frogging made of
velvet rouleaux.

Day outfit, jacket and skirt,
woven wool and mohair mix, printed velvet
Lucile (Lady Duff Gordon). English, 1913-4
Label: Lucile Ltd 23 Hanover Sq, London W1
Worn by Miss Heather Firbank
T.36 & A-1960

THE pocket on Mr
Freedom's brightly coloured artist's smock
is in the form of a bold white satin motif representing an
artist's palette. The smock has long sleeves and fastens at the
front with small pink plastic buttons. It has a 'Bohemian'
long black satin tie knotted at the shirt collar.
The Mr Freedom
label was founded by the fashion entrepreneur
Tommy Roberts who opened his first clothes shop in the King's
Road, Chelsea, London, in September 1969.

Smock, printed cotton, satin appliqué pocket, satin tie.
Mr Freedom. English, July 1971
Label: Mr Freedom presents Pamela Mowtown, Designer
Extraordinaire styled in the modern manner, accept no
substitute. (Cartoon sketch of girl, with word bubble: Look 4
This Label B 4 U Buy). Given by Mr Freedom
T.215-1974

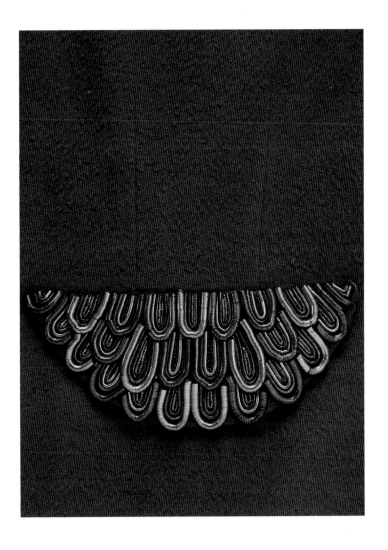

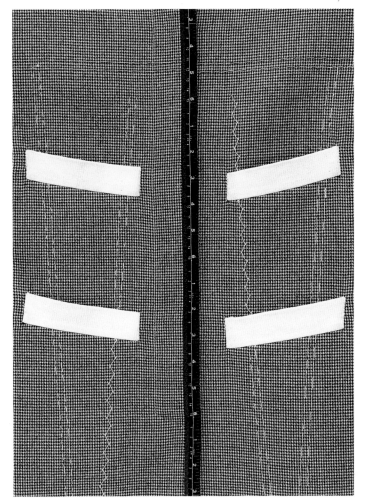

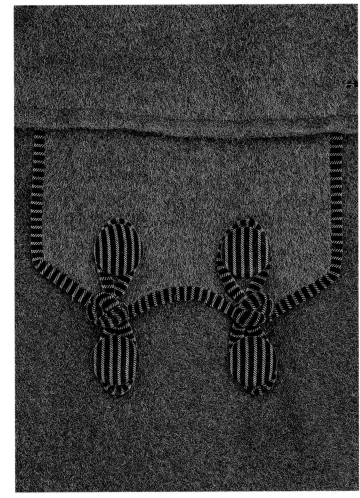

A STRIKINGLY bold,
geometric pattern decorates the generous
collar and turned back cuffs of this loose coat dating from the
early 1900s. In an arresting combination of bright red,
white and black the strong, large scale design is executed in
appliquéd strips of woollen face cloth and bands of black
velvet ribbon encircled by overlapping tubular motifs.
A powerful three dimensional effect is cleverly achieved.
The pattern follows the lines of the wide, deeply notched
shawl collar which has a straight-cut, sailor like back.
A deep, woven braid in gold and black
finishes the edges.

Sweeping the ground,
the woollen top coat fastens with sturdy
hooks and eyes and the convertible collar can be fastened over
to protect the chest. Large, ornate tassels in black silk braid
trim the front and appliqué strips of black satin decorated with
top stitching are applied over the
garment's seams.

In its roomy cut and flowing shape the coat resembles
motoring dust coats or dusters but here, for more formal town
wear, the decoration is highly ornate. The abstract design has a
dynamism which is totally modern in its appeal. A description
of a similar coat in *Our Home* (January, 1904) stresses the
versatility of these unfitted garments; '...For day or evening
wear this kind of coat is very useful because it adapts itself for
many purposes, even in cloth it serves as a comfortable theatre
or evening wrap, and it will also do for visiting wear.'

Coat, woollen cloth,
velvet and satin ribbon. English 1904-7
Given by Miss M C Elliott
T.25-1958

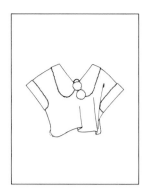

THIS soft, large Peter Pan
collar in natural suede has rounded, pinked edges
and is trimmed with colourful machine appliquéd strips of
leather in a criss-cross pattern. The shaped, two-piece collar is
embellished in the centre with two large pompons in two
shades of brown wool and with brightly
coloured wooden discs.

Using simple
dressmaking techniques with undisguised
machine work, and naturally textured fabrics in unusual
combinations, Pablo & Delia produced a bright and offbeat
look typical of the early 1970s.

Top, felted wool with suede collar and wool pompons
Pablo & Delia. English, 1971
Label: pinked leather, Pablo Delia
T.304-1985

THE distinctive jet
black cuffs of stiffened satin strike a
dramatic contrast against this natural silk duster style coat of
1905-8. The long, unfitted coat is made in undyed tussah silk,
providing a subtle background to the strong black of the
deep turnback cuffs and matching wide shawl collar.
These are highlighted by a delicately embroidered border
of scalloped loops and all-over vermicular infills
in cream floss silk and cord.

Dust coats became fashionable garments in the early
years of this century when travelling by open motor vehicles
on dirt roads became increasingly common.

Dust coat, tussah silk, satin, tulle
English or French, 1905-8. Given by Mrs B White
T.333-1987

THIS imaginative and
romantic 'Renaissance' evening outfit by
Bill Gibb is made from panels of furnishing fabrics in silk
brocade, in pastel shades of pink and blue; it was worn by the
model Twiggy in 1970. Shaped from three separate fabric
pieces, the cuffs fit closely around the wrists and forearms, and
their length is accentuated by seven pink, fabric covered
buttons which fasten through worked buttonholes.
Decorative, glazed cotton panels
at the front and back of the bodice feature figures based upon
Hans Holbein's drawing (about 1520) of heavy and
elaborate costume worn by the wife of a
prosperous citizen of Basle.

Evening outfit, jacket and skirt, silk furnishing fabrics
Bill Gibb. English, 1970. Label: None
Given, and worn by Twiggy at the Daily Mirror Fashion
Celebrity Dinner, 22 October 1970
T.222 to C-1974

A LUMINOUS collar of
silvered kid leather stands out brightly on
this navy, crepe day dress. The Peter Pan collar is pointed at
the front and back and the edges are finished with four rows of
topstitching. A large bow of dark navy velveteen enhances the
collar, while a wide, ruched velvet ribbon runs the
length of the centre front.
The tailored tunic
dress has a simple, fitted bodice which
fastens at the back of the neck with self covered buttons and
loops. The sleeves have puffed shoulders and taper to the wrist with
long darts where the cuffs are secured with snap fasteners.

Day dress, crepe with
kid collar and velveteen bow and trimming
Bought from Boardman's Stratford
English, 1938
Worn and given by Mrs M Burgess
T.239-1973

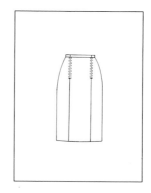

A CLASSIC tailored day
suit in bright scarlet check wool is neatly
finished at collar, cuffs and pockets with Chanel's customary
attention to detail. The semi-fitted, single breasted jacket has
small, square, patch pockets, placed just below the bust and
over the hips. Double lines of topstitching add a crisp finish to
each pocket. They are fastened with small, custom made gilt
buttons, with a leaf design and encircled with scarlet wool.
Straight, set-in, two piece sleeves fasten at the topstitched cuffs
with pairs of gilt buttons. The buttons stand out brightly
against the roughly textured, self-check fabric, which is woven
in two types of wool, glossy and matt. Jacket and skirt are
lined throughout in lightweight scarlet silk. A heavy gilt chain
placed along the inside back hem weights the jacket and
is one of Chanel's distinctive hallmarks.

Chanel pioneered a design philosophy that clothes should be
elegant, comfortable and easy to move in. They were
conceived for the modern woman who wished to appear
absolutely contemporary. Chanel's refreshing and
uncompromising outlook, combined with a dressmaking skill
perfected over many years, never deserted her and enabled
her to make a remarkable comeback in 1954 after an
absence of 15 years.

Chanel suits are now acknowledged to be classics of
international design. Off the body they can appear somewhat
severe and unremarkable but when worn their lines soften and
they are immensely flattering and utterly chic. Chanel had
complete understanding of the female body and her clothes
demonstrated her genius for perfect proportion.

Suit, self check wool
Chanel. French, 1960. Label: Chanel 11676
Worn by the late Mrs Stavros Niarchos and given by
Mr Stavros Niarchos
T.89 & A-1974

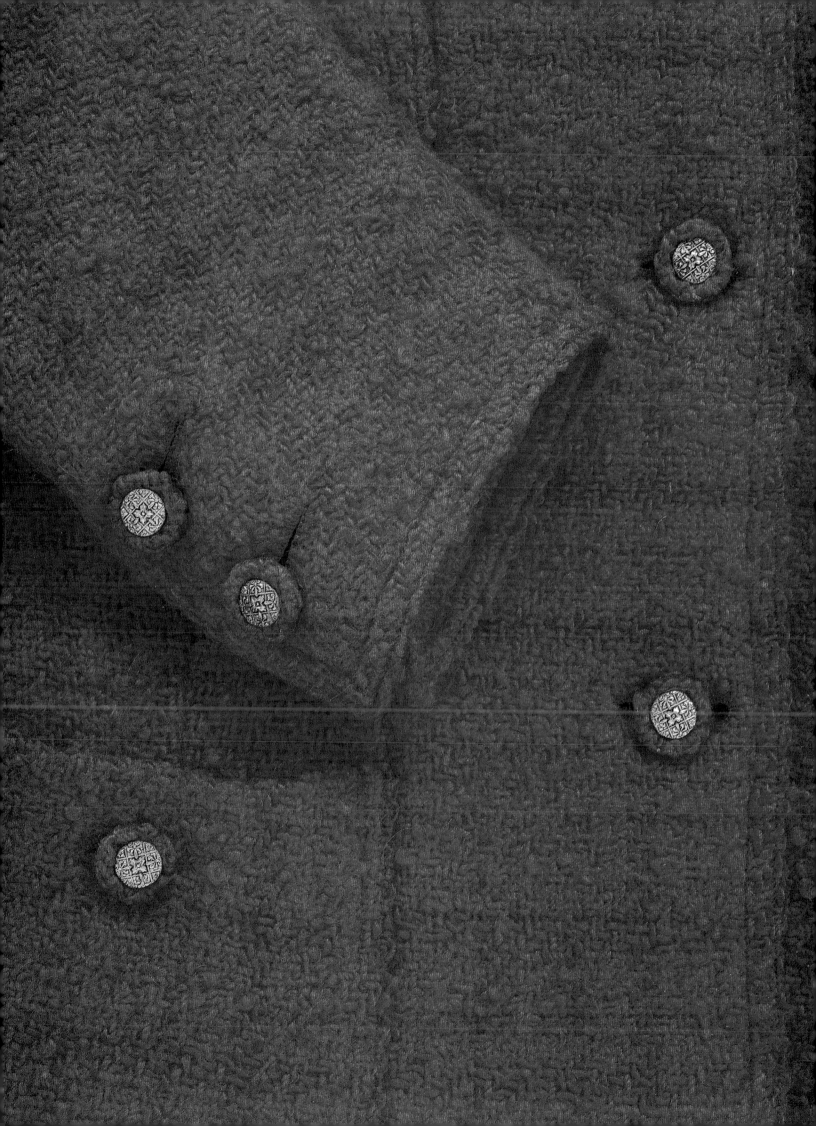

A DEEP border of
fine lace edges the collar and softly falling
jabot of Chanel's cream chiffon blouse. The elegantly foppish
ruffles are gathered into the bodice with small tapering pin-
tucks. The short sleeved blouse, which fastens with gleaming,
round pearl buttons, is entirely hand made and is inset with
vertical panels of lace at back and front, alternating
with rows of narrow pin-tucks.

Chanel is famous for
her suits and chic day wear; perhaps less
well known are her glamorous evening ensembles. The blouse
is part of a sophisticated and striking outfit consisting of a
short, simple tailored bolero jacket and loose, straight, high
waisted trousers, both entirely covered with vertical rows of
overlapping sequins which emphasise the supple, falling lines
of the outfit. The ruffles of delicate lace and chiffon on the
blouse stand out against the shiny, hard sequins, soft
cream contrasting with black. The outfit was originally
finished with a black ribbon tied around the neck,
into which was tucked a red rose.

In adopting the trouser
suit Chanel anticipated the direction
that fashion would again take in the 1960s and 1970s towards
an androgynous look. However, the masculine lines of this
outfit are tempered by the luxurious and sensual textures of
lace and sequins. Chanel said, 'Much seriousness is
required to achieve the frivolous'.

Ensemble, trousers, jacket, covered with black
sequins over silk chiffon and lace blouse with pearl buttons
Chanel. French, 1937-8. Label: none
Worn and given by Mrs Diana Vreeland
T.88 & A-1974

THIS summer 'washing'
dress in crisp lilac and white cotton has
a delicate whitework collar and bow trim. The small, round
white collar is made from fine lawn which has been machine
embroidered in white with a floral design. It is trimmed with a
small tailored double bow in lilac with ends finished by tiny
pendent bobbles in striped cotton. Non-functional buttons
covered in matching striped cotton run the length of the entire
dress. The dress has magyar sleeves made of vertically striped
cotton set deep into the plain lilac bodice, and turn back cuffs
secured with self covered buttons. The flared skirt is cut with
two front and two back panels and a centre back gore
and it is lined with fine lilac silk.

Almost puritanical in
its appeal this dress was worn by Miss
Heather Firbank, who favoured 'exquisite clothes of a heather
colour to complement her name'[1]. The fresh, young style, set
off by the simple whitework collar conjures up pictures of
leisurely summer picnics and boating parties from the
mythologically rosy years before the
First World War.

Summer day dress,
printed cotton with embroidered lawn collar
English, c.1912
Label: Mascotte 89 Park Street Park Lane
Worn by Miss Heather Firbank
T.24-1960

1. Miriam J Benkovitz, *Ronald Firbank: A Biography*,
Weidenfeld and Nicolson, 1970.

THE generous shawl collar
on this bright red New Look suit of 1948 is
unusually shaped at the front in a wide, concave curve.
Two rows of bold black silk braid emphasise the lines of the
collar and continue down the front edges of the jacket. The
collar is cut in one with the jacket fronts forming a soft rolled
shape that extends almost to the shoulders.

The fashionable
curvaceous silhouette of the outfit is formed
by the tightly fitted, unlined hip length jacket and full soft
skirt. The jacket is shaped with panels at back and front which
flare from the waist in a deep peplum, falling in soft folds
around the hips. The hem is edged with a double row of braid
echoing that of the collar. The jacket has long sleeves and
padded shoulders and fastens with round black braid buttons
through worked buttonholes. The gored, mid-calf length skirt
has extra fullness at the back created
by soft pleats.

The bright, strawberry
red, wool and mohair cloth with tiny,
woven, black flecks and heavy, black braid trimming combine
to evoke a military feel. However this is very much softened
by the full skirt and sharply waisted shape of the New Look
style. The outfit was bought for £22 at the Bon Marché store in
Liverpool and was, most unconventionally, worn by the
original owner at her wedding.

Coat and skirt,
woven wool and mohair, with black silk braid
English, 1948. Given by Mrs W Foster
T.14 & A-1960

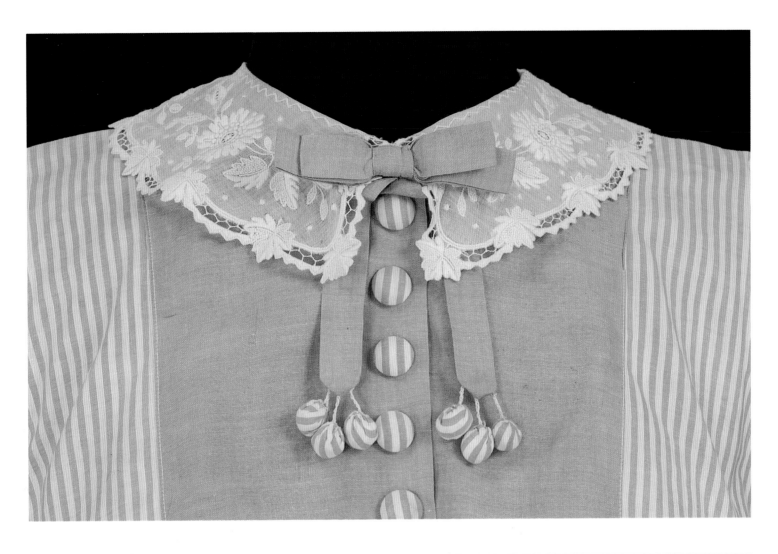

THE stand-up collar of
this silk velvet evening cloak probably
designed by Lucile (Lady Duff Gordon) is formed by three
rows of ruching which draws the malleable fabric into soft
gathers around the neck. High backed, the collar curves gently
down at the front where it fastens with a single hook and eye
and its base is trimmed with plump, pink satin rose buds with
three large buds at the back and six smaller versions at the
front. The rose-pink velvet has a bold voided design of stylised
flowering rose stems and leaves which emphasises the
floral theme of this luxurious garment.

Long and unfitted the cloak is double layered,
with an outer cloak falling from the shoulders in graceful folds
to a broadly scalloped hem at hip level. The inner layer is
formed from the pink satin lining, gathered into the neck and
then seamed at waist level to a velvet panel which falls to the
ground and finishes with a wide scalloped hem.

Romantically inclined,
Lady Duff Gordon's delight in pliant
fabrics in pastel colours is well documented in her
autobiography, 'wearing a dress of soft grey chiffon veiling an
underdress of shot pink and violet taffeta. It looked rather like
an opal, and gave the impression of something shadowed and
unreal'[1]. Like John Galliano's wedding coat of 60 years later,
this pretty, feminine cloak uses fabric flowers to enhance and
adorn. In this case they draw attention to the soft and
flattering collar which was formed to frame
the wearer's face.

Evening cloak, silk velvet, satin roses
Probably Lucile. English, c.1915
Given by Mr Vern Lambert
T.298-1974

1. Lady Duff Gordon, *Discretions and
Indiscretions*, Jarrolds, 1932.

BUTTONS

BUTTONS featured on this
tailored ensemble bear a war-time message.
The design for the jacket, skirt and blouse
was commissioned by the Board of Trade from the
Incorporated Society of London Fashion Designers, as one of
32 Utility outfits intended for general production. *Vogue*
featured the collection in October 1942; 'All the designs are, of
course, within the New Austerity specifications: only so many
buttons, this much cuff and that much skirt ... but they are an
object lesson in the power of pure style over mere elegance'.
The ensemble is in grey, white and red herringbone tweed and
the illustrated blouse has a rust-red, grosgrain
ribbon bow tying at the neck.

Both jacket and blouse fasten with three buttons, the
maximum number allowed under Utility regulations. The
bronze coloured metal has the Utility symbol, CC41, which
stands for 'Civilian Clothing', and '1941'. The symbol was
designed by Reginald Schipp, who was asked to disguise the
'CC', 'so that the public should not recognise the letters as
such'[1]. The stylised motif became known as 'the cheeses'. The
buttons were produced in two sizes and are backed by
conventional plastic buttons with shanks.

These functional buttons form a significant detail on the
restrained, tailored outfit. In utilising the CC41 symbol they
make the most of the minimal decorative opportunities
allowed. In type they belong to that group of buttons which
designers sign with their own initials. Such logo buttons are
multi-purpose and while being highly decorative can also
impart a message or advertise their designer.

Herringbone tweed
ensemble with metal buttons (2.5 and 2 cm
in diameter). Digby Morton. English, Autumn 1942
Label: No 16 Original DM 92/10' (Handwritten paper tag
indicating maximum selling price of just under £5.00 or $8.50)
Given by the Board of Trade
T.45 to B1942

1. *Utitlity Furniture and Fashion 1941-51,*
Geffrye Museum, ILEA, 1974.

ROWS of small,
prettily embroidered buttons provide a
decorative touch on this mauve satin indoor wrap. The
wooden core of each button is covered with matching satin and
worked with mauve-grey twisted silk thread in a spider's web
pattern. The buttons fasten the loosely draped wrap at the
neck, hip and cuffs with fine silk loops, shaped from a
continuous length of braid. Although the garment was
purchased from Russell & Allen, one of the great London
stores of the Edwardian period, the buttons are similar to
many home embroidered examples made to answer demand in
an era of expansion in the haberdashery business.

The silk chiffon lining,
shown as a background to the cuff, is
patterned with flowers in delicate shades of mauve and grey on
a black ground. This is a simple garment which relies for its
impact upon the soft, draping quality of the pastel coloured
satin, an occasional glimpse of pretty linen and the fine
detailing of the delicately worked buttons.

Satin wrap with self-covered buttons
English, 1918-20
Label: Russell & Allen Old Bond St London W1
Worn by Miss Heather Firbank
T.46-1960

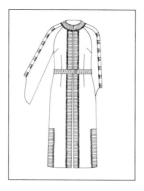 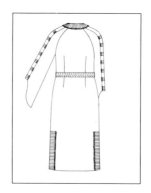

BRIGHT red, wooden
buttons and numerous parallel rows of
braid create a bold, purely decorative pattern on this black
satin overdress. Wide, scarlet satin bands are placed on the
high neck, bodice, raglan sleeves and side vents to form a
vibrant base for the closely overlaid lengths of narrow, black
braid. Each of these is secured at one end by a minute round
button (diameter 10 mm), attached through its single, central
hole with black thread, carefully positioned to create
part of the linear design.

In this dress, a tiny detail is repeated to create an
arresting, geometric pattern in striking colours, achieving an
almost military look. The strong contrast of red against black
is further enhanced by the intense sheen of the early rayon
fabric. Machine made wooden buttons were an inexpensive
alternative to ivory, bone and shell which had become scarce in
Europe after the First World War and these cheaper substitutes
could therefore be used in considerable quantity.
This overdress was probably made by a good local or
home dressmaker with a flair for the unusual and the
highly decorative.

Rayon overdress, with braid and wooden buttons
Maker unknown. German, 1920s
Given by Miss U H Giedke in memory of her friend
Mrs Bruno Lewin
T.273 & A-1988

EYE-LIKE buttons peer out from the green, white
and orange dappling on Ungaro's camouflage patterned coat
and skirt. Matching buttons are made from a circular, matt
green base with a raised and shaped matt white overlay. Tiny
splashes of orange pick up the colour of the sun-like discs in
the bold, printed fabric. The outfit, with matching orange
suede waistcoat, was illustrated in *Vogue* of September 1968,
which exhorted its readers to '... change to a pretty
camouflage print, Ungaro does, he uses Nattier's blurred
jungle green stripes with orange suns'.

The buttons fasten the double breasted front of the short,
flared coat and trim the pockets and vestigial half-belt. To
convey Ungaro's dedicated and meticulous attention to even
the smallest detail, part of the coat's centre back is illustrated.
The half-belt, centre seam and deep inverted pleat are carefully
cut to align the complex, organic printed pattern, and the
custom made buttons provide a final
enigmatic touch.

Printed woollen coat and skirt with plastic composition
buttons and suede waistcoat
Emanuel Ungaro (fabric designed by Sonia Knapp,
made by Nattier). French, Autumn 1968
Label: Emanuel Ungaro Couture Paris
Given and worn by Mrs Brenda Azario
T.314 to B-1978

FOUR acrobat buttons
leap from a bright pink, fitted jacket by
Schiaparelli. The silk twill has a repeating pattern of rearing
horses woven in two shades of blue; their saddles, manes and
plumes picked out in metallic thread. Specially designed, both
fabric and buttons were made for Schiaparelli's Circus
Collection of 1938, in which the featured jacket was worn with
a dark purple crepe evening dress with draped culotte hem. It
was '... the most riotous and swaggering fashion show that
Paris had ever seen'[1] with 'a million novelty effects ...
prancing dogs and horses, grey elephants, spotlit
acrobats, tents and clowns'[2].

Schiaparelli commissioned extravagant and decorative
buttons as important points of detail for her distinctive outfits.
These hand made, cast metal acrobats are full of vitality and
humour and their movement is equalled by that of the
prancing pairs of horses. Painted pale pink and blue, the large
and extremely heavy buttons are attached through the cloth in
a novel way, with small, brass screws connecting with large
slide hooks and eyes. Buttons played an essential role in
Schiaparelli's art, 'King Button still reigned without fear at
Schiap's. The most incredible things were used, animals and
feathers, caricatures and paper-weights, chains, locks, clips,
and lollipops. Some were of wood and others of plastic, but
not one looked like what a button was
supposed to look like'[3].

Silk twill jacket with cast metal buttons (6.5 cm long)
Elsa Schiaparelli. French, February 1938
Given by Miss Ruth Ford and worn by her mother
T.395 & A-1974

1. *Elsa Schiaparelli,* Palmer White, Rizzoli, 1986, p. 166.
2. *Hommage á Elsa Schiaparelli,* Musée de la Mode
et du Costume, 1984, p. 46.
3. Elsa Schiaparelli, *Shocking Life,* J.M. Dent & Sons, 1954 p. 98.

TINY, bee shaped buttons fasten the bodice of
this pale blue evening dress. The sweeping, romantic gown was
bought in 1972 to wear as a wedding dress. Bill Gibb's
personal 'signature' motif was a bee and it appears on many
outfits he designed in the form of embroidered and appliquéd
details, belt clasps and buttons. These particular metal bees are
enamelled in black and yellow stripes with white wings
fastening through machine-worked buttonholes. Precision
made, they stand out clearly against the plain moss crepe
fabric, providing a jewel-like focus.

The front and back bodice of this dress has double
topstitched seams, echoing the rows of alternating black and
yellow topstitching on the flared cuffs, collar and hem, and
picking up the bee colours. Long dolman sleeves button at the
wrist with three additional bees which fasten through
loops in matching fabric.

A similar dress,
but in ivory, was described as 'Bill Gibb's
Evening Spectacular' in *Vogue*, October 1972; 'a satin back
crepe dress ... amazing multi-gored skirt, dolman sleeves
narrowing to medieval points, black and yellow stitching to
blend with bee buttons. £70'. Bill Gibb was well known for his
lavish evening wear. He said 'I have to stick to what I do best,
to my own style, which is rich both in
fabrics and detail'[1].

Moss crepe evening
dress with enamelled metal buttons
Bill Gibb. English, 1972. Label: Bill Gibb London
Given by Mrs Angela Dixon
T.172-1986

1. *The Guardian*, Thursday May 20 1982, p. 11:
'Expensive thrills', Brenda Polan.

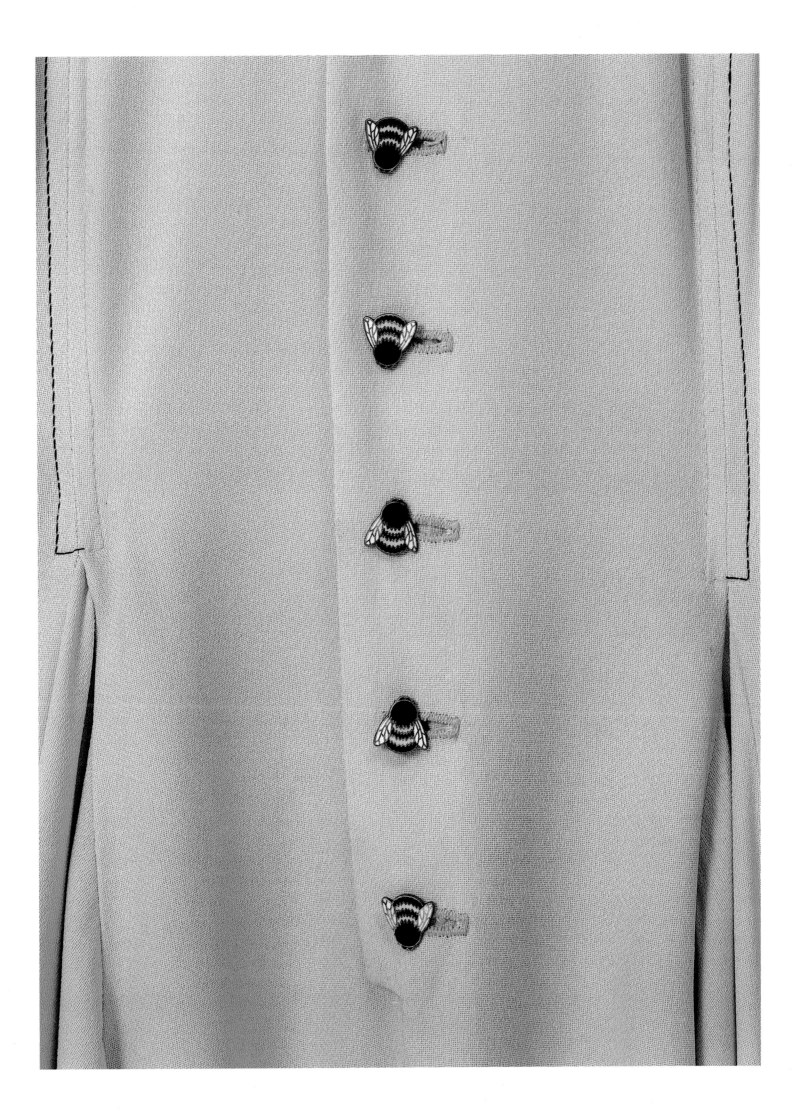

A PAIR of unusual, coiled
straw buttons emphasises the shaped,
cross-over bodice of this cool, black linen summer dress of
about 1948. The entire skirt is also embellished with regularly
placed, matching buttons. They are made from fine, plaited
straw strips rolled into tight, neat spirals and secured with
thread. The light, natural colour of the straw stands out in
contrast against the smooth black linen, transforming an
artfully cut, but plain dress into an inventively trimmed and
striking garment. The buttons on the bodice perform a
function in securing the cross-over panels and convey the idea
of operational fastenings by the inclusion of false bound
buttonholes but neither they, nor those on the skirt, had to
withstand the wear and tear of daily use. As a result, the straw
coils remain in pristine condition, despite being fragile and
perishable. Use of such an unconventional and cheap material
was probably a legacy from the war-time shortages of more
lavish trimmings and fabrics of high fashion.

Jacques Heim was
one of the first top designers to investigate
the potential of ready-to-wear. This dress has historical
significance because it is a rare and early model from his ready-
made range, Heim Actualité.

Linen day dress with straw buttons (3 cm in diameter)
Jacques Heim. French, c.1948
Label: Heim Actualité Cannes Paris Biarritz
Given by Miss Catherine Hunt and worn by
Miss Martita Hunt
T.117-1970

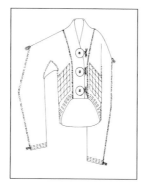 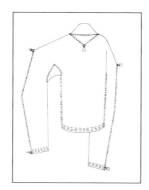

THIS 'kitchen sink'
cardigan by Vivienne Westwood is made in
loosely woven, dishcloth cotton, dyed purple. Its singular look
is completed by three huge, burnished metal buttons, which
are made from 'Vim' scouring powder lids. Each lid is attached
with coloured cotton thread through the ready-punched holes
and fastens with a loop of thick cotton cord, which is knotted
and left to unravel at the ends. The cardigan has two, square,
patch pockets constructed from interwoven strips of pink,
green, yellow and purple dishcloth. Long, off-the-shoulder
sleeves gather at the wrist with three rows of coloured cotton
cord and the shoulders and back are decorated with fluffy
tassels. The exposed seams and oversized style, cut on the flat,
run concurrently with the successful Japanese look of the
early '80s. Vivienne Westwood said at the time:

'What I'm not
trying to do with my clothes is to make a kind
of shell that stays in place half an inch away from the body.
My clothes are dynamic. They pull and they push and they
slightly fall off. There's more to clothes than just comfort.
Even if they're not quite comfortable and slip and have to be
readjusted now and again I don't mind, because that's some
sort of display and gesture that belongs
with the clothes'[1]

Vivienne Westwood's
provocative and individual approach 'undermining the status
system of fashion'[2] is humorously summed up here by the use
of an everyday
domestic product.

Woven cotton cardigan with
'distressed' metal buttons. (7.5 cm in diameter)
Vivienne Westwood. English, c.1982
Label: Worlds End McLaren Westwood
Born in England
T.366-1985

1. *The Times,* Tuesday, August 23 1983, p 7,
'The shock of the new', Georgina Howell.
2. Ibid.

BOWS

THE dominating feature of Victor Steibel's striped silk grosgrain dress of Autumn 1947 is the enormous bustle bow at the rear, an unusually extravagant touch for day wear. So large and weighty is the bow that it requires the support of a sturdy horsehair frill beneath the skirts. The lavish use of material for a decorative, non-functional trimming was a defiant gesture in this time of austerity and rationing.

The fitted bodice
fastens along the centre front with three
black glass buttons and has a large collar, short sleeves and padded shoulders. A fashionably bouffant skirt is supported by spreading net petticoats and the waist is gathered on the outside with rows of shirring, the selvedge used to create a crisp finish. Beneath the nets a slightly longer, straight underskirt in matching grosgrain with the stripes placed vertically creates optical contrasts and a layered effect, revealing Steibel's known talent for clever manipulation of striped fabrics.

The New Look,
launched by Christian Dior in February 1947,
featured pinched waists, long full skirts and a soft shoulder line. The impractical scale and frivolity of this bow lends support to recent interpretations of the New Look as a post-war reaction to the utilitarian garb women were confined to during the war years. It can be seen as an attempt to reinstate femininity in dress after a period of austerity and shortage.

Day dress, silk grosgrain with self fabric bow
Victor Steibel. English, Autumn 1947
Label: Victor Steibel at Jacqmar 16, Grosvenor Street,
London, W1. Given by Lady Cornwallis
T.292-1984

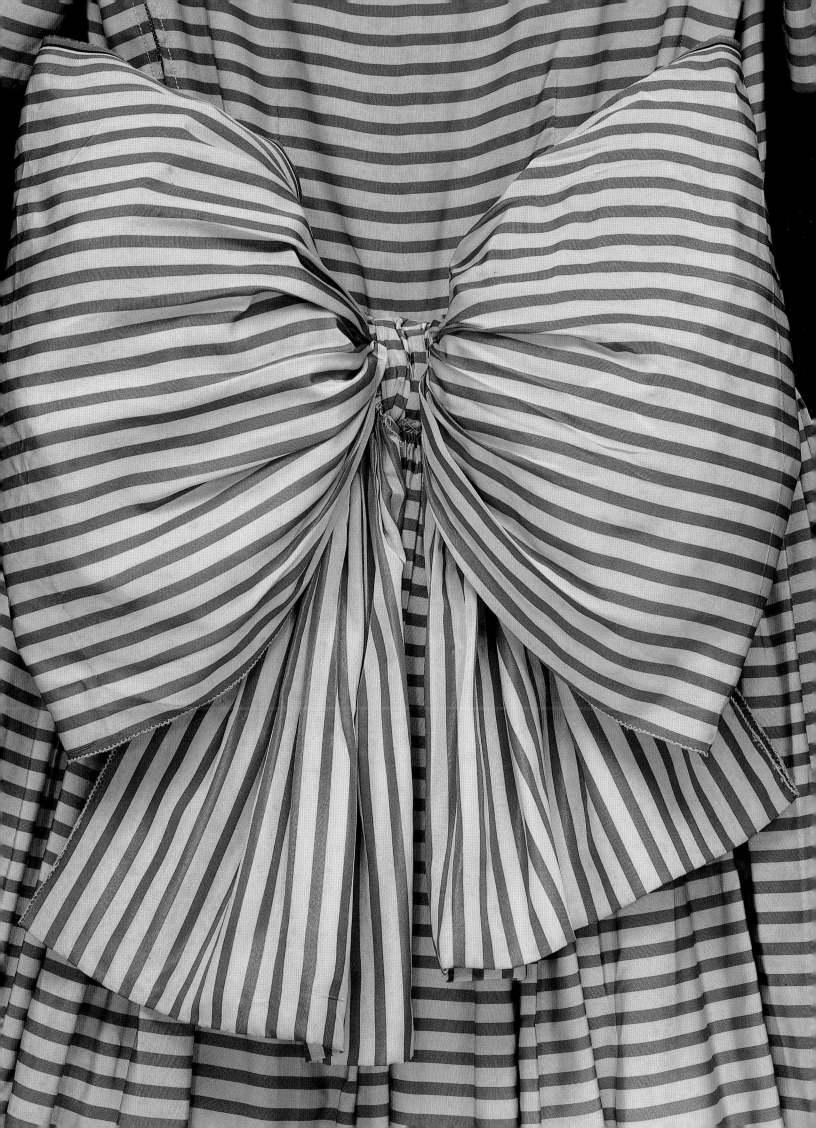

BLACK is used in
a series of contrasts of matt and shiny
materials in this sparkling evening dress by Yves Saint Laurent
for Christian Dior. The confection of tulle is embellished with
a scattering of tiny jet beads and a series of black satin bows.
The untailored bows are tied in 3 cm wide ribbon and are used
to punctuate the gathered swags of tulle which cover the belled
skirt. Additional bows provide finishing details down the
bodice centre front. The bows with their cut ribbon ends left
raw, lend a soft and romantic touch to this highly
sophisticated couture garment.

The dress depends upon a boned corset foundation and
numerous stiffened net and horsehair petticoats, amounting to
a weighty structure that almost stands up on its own. Over the
foundation the net bodice fastens with press studs above which
tiny nonfunctional buttons are placed, each trimmed with a
single jet bead. The scallop edged neck and translucent raglan
sleeves are trimmed with rows of matching beads. The full
skirt is arranged in gracefully swagged tulle, the gathers
increasing in scale from waist to hem. All these applied details,
delicately imposed upon the garment, combine to create a
glistening, fairy-tale dress.

Evening dress, silk
tulle, jet with satin ribbon bows. Christian Dior
French, Spring/Summer 1959
Label: Christian Dior Paris Made In France no. 94460
Worn and given by the Duchess of Windsor
T.125-1974

THIS simple 'sea-side frock'
of about 1912 has as its focal point a
large, spotted, silk twill cravat which is loosely tied in a bow
to fasten the bodice front. Such cravats or foulards were
popular at the time on blouses as well as dresses and were
often interchangeable. They were inspired by earlier masculine
neck-wear. *The Queen* in August 1912 described 'the prettiest
style of Robespierre collar, finishing with a Latin Quartier
cravat of blue and white birdseye spot silk'.

Almost puritanical in its appeal, the dress is made in sky blue
slubbed 'washing' linen. The bodice has a high V-neck and
long kimono style sleeves which are joined by delicate
faggoting along the dropped shoulder seams. Two large
pockets with long, curved edges are set in low at the sides.
Crisp, white, organza cuffs with picot edging match the deep
collar which sets off the soft and generous
silk bow to perfection.

Fresh and young
in its appeal this garment presents a less
formal side of Miss Heather Firbank's wardrobe from which
several garments are shown in this book and would have been
worn for morning activities or for summer holiday leisure
pursuits. Although of a similar date this jaunty spotted bow is
in complete contrast to the lavish bow featured on the back of
the sophisticated evening gown (plate 51).

Day dress, linen with
silk organza collar and cuffs and silk twill bow
English, c.1912-14
Worn by Miss Heather Firbank
T.17-1960

THIS expensive watered
silk with its shimmering and reflective
surface reveals a subtle, damask-woven pattern of tiny ribbon
bows – a fanciful and light touch on a full and elaborate
evening coat of 1903.

The cream-toned French silk, probably made in Lyons,
has the watered appearance characteristic of moiré, an effect
which is achieved in the finishing process where the finely
ribbed silk is compressed between heated, engraved copper
rollers, producing an irregular rippled effect. As light moves
over the surface of the cloth, it reveals a fluid
background to the dancing bows.

Evening coat, silk moiré with woven
bows, lace and embroidery. Possibly Worth
French, c.1903. Given by Mrs J Allenby
T.66-1966

THE strategically
placed half-bow on this bright green and
black mini-dress emphasises the wearer's movement
in an arresting and humorous way.
Lacroix is famed for his
eclecticism and this example from one of his
earliest collections marries the mini-dress with a bustle-
like flounce borrowed from 19th century costume. He said
'Every one of my dresses possesses a detail that can be
connected with something historic, something from a
past culture. We don't invent anything'[1].

Evening dress, silk satin with satin
flounce and bow. Christian Lacroix. French, 1987-8
Label: Christian Lacroix Lux Paris
T.246-1989

1. *Vogue*, March 1988.

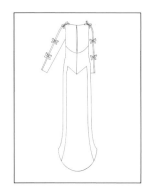

SILK taffeta ribbon bows
trim the shoulders and sleeves of Eva Lutyens'
cerise, rippled crepe, evening dress. The demure, bi-
coloured bows are tied in neat, picot edged ribbons in pastel
shades of green and pink, in combination with maroon. The
bows secure the sleeves and shoulders together, holding the
dress onto the body, and giving tantalising glimpses of the
bare arms beneath. This seductive effect is furthered
by the revealingly open back.
The clinging, full length crepe
dress is ingeniously cut and requires a minimal
amount of fastening, with a single hook and eye at the neck back.
The front skirt, sides and midriff are cut in one, with a curved
central back panel forming the main part of the small train.

Evening dress, crepe with silk ribbon bows
Eva Lutyens. English, late 1930s. Label: Eva Lutyens London
Given by Martin Kamer
T.105-1988

THIS pink satin bow
provides an elegant final touch to Pierre
Balmain's glamorous sheath style evening dress. The bow is
placed in the small of the back where satin sash and draped
skirt meet in a series of asymmetrical, diagonal gathers.
The pearl white satin fabric of the dress is shot with silver
metallic threads and woven with a pattern of small thistles and
painstakingly hand painted in pastel shades, while the strapless
bodice is embellished with leaves appliquéd with minute
stitches. The dress is a tiny size 6 and was worn by the
Austrian film star Lilli Palmer in the 1956 film
Teufel im Seide (Devil in Silk).

Evening dress, satin woven
with metallic thread, hand painted, and satin bow
Pierre Balmain. French, c.1956. Label: Pierre Balmain Paris
Worn and given by Miss Lilli Palmer
T.252-1981

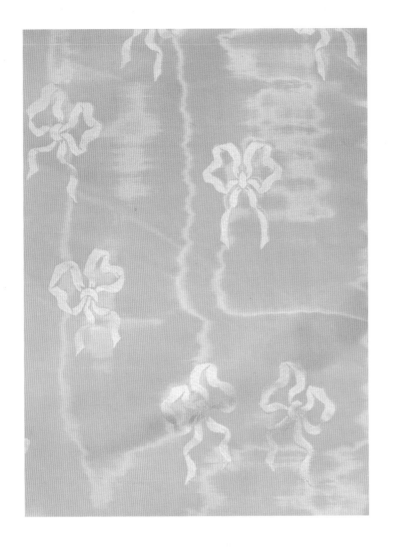

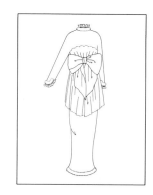

THIS highly fashionable reception gown of about
1912 was worn by Miss Heather Firbank. The Victoria and
Albert Museum acquired a collection of Miss Firbank's clothes
after they had been discovered packed in trunks where they
had lain for almost 35 years. The gown culminates in a wide,
high waisted sash in bias cut, ivory satin, tying behind in an
enormous butterfly bow. The bow is exceptionally wide and
falls to below the hips, which must have been slightly
awkward for the wearer. Sitting was probably limited to
perching on the edge of a chair. By 1914 *The Queen* journal
had disapprovingly declared that widespread fad for such
'mammoth' butterfly bows would not last, as 'their
presence is too easily acquired' [1].

The bow is entirely
decorative, for the dress is actually secured
by a series of complex, hidden fastenings, with numerous tiny
hooks and eyes. The bow belies an outward impression of
softness and pliability for it is lined with stiff organza and
wired at the edges to retain its shape. Like the firmly corseted
figure below the diaphanous gown, the bow is very
deliberately structured with the
aid of rigid materials.

The bodice and sleeves of the dress are cut in one piece, in
ivory chiffon over cream tulle. A silk machine-lace panel
attached at the bust forms the overtunic which is gathered at
the waist and falls in soft folds to the hips. The high frilled
neck, narrow cuffs and draped, divided skirt are edged with
brown skunk fur which was very fashionable at that time. *The
Queen* noted that 'fur softens everything, allied with chiffon'.
The dress is possibly by Lucile, the society dressmaker, who
was well known for her feminine designs, delicate use of
colour and fine dressmaking detail.

Afternoon or reception gown, silk, satin, tulle, machine lace
and skunk fur, with satin bow
Possibly Lucile (Lady Duff Gordon). English, c.1912-14
Worn by Miss Heather Firbank
T.34-1960

1. Quoted and illustrated by Janet Arnold, *Patterns of
Fashion 2*, new edition 1977, p. 62.

PHILIPPE Venet
explores the bow theme in this arresting evening dress in black
and white silk. An enormous, cape-like collar of stiffened
white silk organza stands wide of the shoulders, falling mid-
way to the waist. Dramatically, it is threaded at front and
shoulders with a generous black satin sash which ties at the
back in a huge butterfly bow. In addition a profusion of small,
embroidered bow-shaped motifs are lightly appliquéd over the
dress, their free-standing edges creating an animated, fluttering
effect that contrasts with the static gravity of the
single bow above.

The dress is made in black silk with self-woven
large spots, and further textured with tiny machine
embroidered dots in white. It is floor length, sleeveless and
simply cut, with a high straight neck and gathered waist. Venet
uses bows in the form of a singular, three-dimensional feature
and as an applied, repeated motif pattern, contrasting scale and
texture within a simple black and white palette. The result is a
commanding evening gown with theatrical impact
from both front and back.

Evening dress, silk, organza and satin
Philippe Venet. French, 1989
Label: Philippe Venet Paris
T.190-1990

TWO softly tailored bows
form the finishing touch to Christian
Dior's feminine evening dress of 1957. Precisely placed either
side of the bodice, the bows draw attention to the flattering,
cross-over décolletage. The confidently large bows are made to
match the dress in a deep, crushed raspberry coloured satin
organza and appear to hold the soft gathers of the material
together as it flows from the deep, falling collar into
the closely fitting bodice.

Dior wrote that 'Many
a dress of mine is born of the fabric
alone' [1]. He manipulates the luxurious, crisp, satin weave to
great effect. The bodice, collar and bows are integrated into
the fluidly gathered and shaped form, complemented by the
simple skirt. Full and short, its bouffant shape is pleated into
the tight waist and supported by four layers of net petticoat
beneath, the innermost reinforced by
horsehair stiffening.

Cecil Beaton called Christian Dior 'the Watteau of
dressmaking – full of nuances, chic, delicate and timely' [2].

Evening dress, satin organza with self fabric bows
Christian Dior. English, 1957
Label: Christian Dior UK Regd Made in England by
Christian Dior Ltd London 13445
Worn and given by Mrs William Mann
T.235-1985

1. Christian Dior, *Talking
about Fashion*, Hutchinson & Co, 1954, p 40.
2. Cecil Beaton, *The Glass of Fashion*, Weidenfeld
& Nicolson, 1954, p. 259.

ELSA Schiaparelli plays
with the idea of a bow in this *trompe
l'oeil* woollen jumper, designed in 1927. The simple, hand
knitted garment and its direct, graphic image point to a more
relaxed attitude to informal wear for women. Schiaparelli's is
not the feminine, fussy bow of the past but a confident and
jaunty motif for the new woman of the 1920s.

The geometric, 'stepped' quality of the bow's curved
outlines are an unavoidable technical feature of hand knitting;
the designer exploits this stylisation, eschewing naturalism in
favour of an emblematic image which hints at her later
involvement with the Surrealist movement. 'I drew a large
butterfly bow in front, like a scarf round the neck –
a primitive drawing of a child …' [1].

Schiaparelli wore the jumper to a society luncheon where it
was a remarkable success, leading to numerous orders. More
designs for amusing knitwear followed, depicting for example
trompe l'oeil ties and handkerchiefs. The first Schiaparelli salon
opened soon after, selling modish sportswear. Like many of
the designer's later ideas, the success of this jumper came from
her understanding of the fashionable potential of traditional
craftwork – in this case, knitting – allied to her own
considerable inventiveness and wit.

Hand knitted woollen jumper Elsa Schiaparelli
French, 1927. Given by Madame Elsa Schiaparelli
T.388-1974

1. Elsa Schiaparelli, *Shocking Life,* J M Dent & Sons, 1954

BEADS & SEQUINS

THIS short sleeved
evening jacket designed by Mainbocher
illustrates the classic, late 1930s silhouette of nipped-in waist
and wide, padded shoulders. The garment also has details
which are typical of the period: turn-back cuffs and a large,
pointed collar. This uncomplicated, tailored, matt silk jacket is
used as a vehicle for a stunning, sequinned Chinoiserie design.
The highly reflective, brilliantly coloured sequins are laid
down in overlapping densely packed rows composing the
floral and foliate design. The pattern does not cover the surface
of the entire jacket and the unreflective black ground is
used as a foil to the glowing colours.

All details, no
matter how small, count in high fashion and a
pleasing touch is that the four buttons which fasten the front
are sequinned to match the jacket.

Mainbocher was the
first American designer to open a couture
house in Paris and is probably best known for the elegant
clothes he created for the Duchess of Windsor. This evening
jacket numbers among the last Mainbocher designs made in
Paris. At the outbreak of World War II he closed the house
and eventually re-opened in New York.

Evening jacket, sequinned silk
Mainbocher. Paris 1939
Worn and given by Lady Beit
T.309-1974

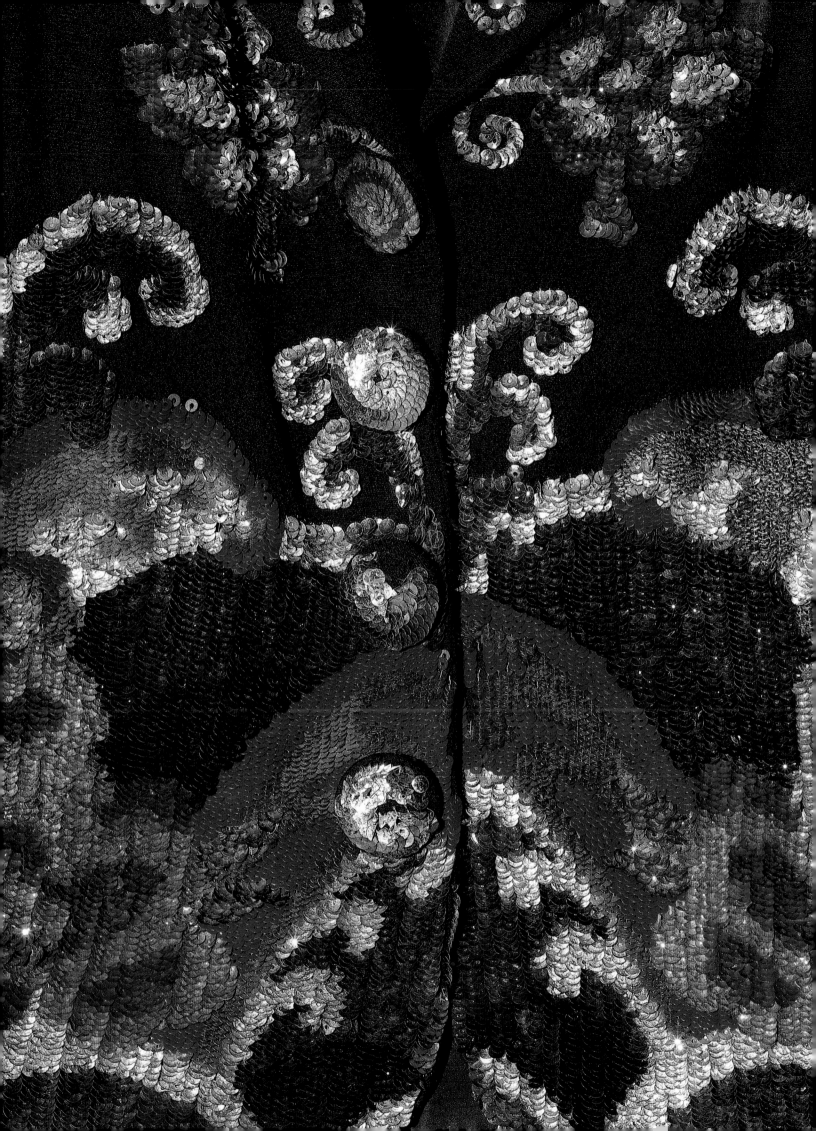

THIS voluptuous evening
dress, sequinned all over, encloses the
body like a glistening second skin. Silver sequins, backed with
gold, overlap to provide a fluid and rippling fishscale surface
that reflects surrounding light and colour. The sequins are
carefully aligned to emphasise the structure of the bodice
which has a draped front formed by two flared ties
which curve around the sides to fasten at the back.

Full length and
sleeveless, the dress is made in deep blue tulle
onto which the sequins are tamboured. It has a low, wide
V-shaped front neck and plunge back with wide straps.

Evening dress, sequinned tulle
French or English, 1935/6. Given by The Dowager
Countess of Pembroke and Montgomery, CBE
T.343-1960

THREE-DIMENSIONAL,
sparkling, pendant tassels with fringes of
tiny, silvered glass beads hang beside a pair of two-
dimensional, brocaded tassels on a silver evening dress of 1919.
Tassels were an extremely popular decorative motif at this time
and here the designer wittily juxtaposes a flat, *trompe l'oeil*
image, with real tassels.

Evening dress,
brocaded silk with diamanté, beaded
motifs and tassels of silvered beads and diamanté
Reville and Rossiter. English, 1919
Label: Court Dressmakers Reville & Rossiter Ltd
Hanover Square W1. Worn by the Hon
Mrs Pearson for her 1922 portrait. Given by
Lord and Lady Cowdray
T.199-1970

SUMPTUOUS gold and
white beadwork encrusts this ivory
Duchesse satin, state evening dress designed by Norman
Hartnell and worn by HRM Queen Elizabeth on a state visit
to Paris in 1957. The dazzling, jewel-like detail of the 'flowers
of the fields of France' design, includes grasses, wheat and wild
flowers worked in relief in faceted glass stones, gold beads,
brilliants and variously shaped pearls, with mother-of-pearl
and cloth of gold petals. The miniature bees (inspired by
Napoleon's personal emblem) are of gold twisted thread with
iridescent pearl wings and beaded antennae.

State evening dress, embroidered Duchesse satin
Norman Hartnell. English 1957
Worn by Her Majesty the Queen on the State visit to Paris,
April 1957, for the banquet at the Elysée Palace followed by
the Opera. Given by HM the Queen.
T.264-1974

A SIMPLE, sleeveless
mini-dress by Yves Saint Laurent is
encrusted all over with sequins and long, curving paillettes.
The off-white cigaline bodice is covered with randomly
applied pearl white sequins and scattered paillettes and its neck
and armholes are edged with diamanté strip and crystal beads.
White sequins shade to embossed silver, then to gunmetal grey
and to a thicket of black sequins and spiky paillettes.

Evening dress, cigaline,
sequins, paillettes and ostrich feathers
Yves Saint Laurent (cigaline by Bucol, embroidery by
Vermont). French, autumn-winter 1967
Label: Yves Saint Laurent Made in France 017254
Worn and given by Princess Stanislaus Radziwill
T.368-1974

 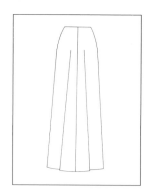

A HIGHLY coloured,
floral pattern adorns the corsage of
this plum velvet evening jacket designed by Schiaparelli.
Fronds and leaves are worked in bronze and gold coloured fine
metallic threads and bright metal strips. Blue and pink oval
glass rhinestones form stylised flower heads. They have been
facetted and claw set to emulate real jewels. In addition, tiny
blue and gold sequins are scattered over the jacket which
fastens with three, large, pink, embossed metal buttons
resembling flowers. The rich golds of the baroque design are
set off by the deep hue of the silk velvet.

In her energetic pursuit
of effective design Schiaparelli was
inspired by a range of historical and traditional embroideries
including magnificently embroidered ecclesiastical vestments.
Here, she '... returned to the use of embroidery materials
employed centuries before ... and asked for designs recalling
liturgical ornamentation of the 16th century'.[1]

Schiaparelli used a
formally tailored ensemble as the perfect
foil for her gloriously adventurous
embroideries.

Evening ensemble,
silk velvet, rhinestones, sequins and gilt
threads. Elsa Schiaparelli. French 1938
Worn and given by Lady Trevor Roper, now
Lady Dacre of Glanton.
T.398+A-1974

1. Palmer White,
Haute Couture Embroidery, the Art of Lesage.
The Vendome Press 1988

NEON coloured sequins
cover the entire surface of this leotard
in a vibrant, flowing paisley design. The sequins are tamboured
on to a black organza base in a dense overlapping manner. The
pink, blue, and yellow pattern is outlined with black and
lightly scattered with ruby coloured and clear glass beads.
Sleeveless and close fitting, the maillot has a high round neck,
deeply cut away armholes and fastens
with a zip at the side.

This alluring ensemble
shows another side of Madame Grès
who is normally associated with highly refined, draped and
pleated classic evening gowns. Here, a snazzily sequinned
'bathing costume' is worn beneath an almost monastic
overdress save that its top is translucent black organza
through which the sequinned leotard glistens and sparkles.
The overdress is a remarkable concept with its flowing
bishop sleeves and yoke top in frail organza bearing the
immense weight of the huge velvet circle that forms
the floor length skirt.

Evening outfit, organza,
velvet, sequins, faceted glass beads
Madame Grès. French, 1965
Label: Gres, 1 Rue de la Paix Made in France
Given by Madame Grès
T.248 & A-1974

THIS vivid orange
silk velvet 'flapper' dress has a skirt of
orange and peach velvet streamers, lightly beaded along the
edges. The streamers are arranged in three staggered rows
oversewn to the dress with bright yellow and peach floss silk
thread. Each streamer tapers to a slender point and is lined
with bright yellow silk. The gold bugle beads which trim and
weight the edges, form a delicate, hanging fringe and
emphasise the linear style of the dress.

Elaborately beaded
and fringed dance dresses were *de rigueur* in the mid to late
1920s. Fringes were especially popular as they responded to
every step, exaggerating and drawing attention to the dancer's
movements. Likewise ornate beadwork was widely used as, in
motion, beads caught the light and glittered in a beguiling way.
It was a time when popular, energetic dances, especially the
Charleston, required short skirts which left the legs free – this
particular design would have been ideal for
such hectic activity.

This dress was worn
by Miss Emilie Grigsby, a wealthy and
independent society hostess whose 'pale beauty and golden
hair' [1] must have looked striking in this exuberant garment so
redolent of the jazz age.

Evening dress and belt, silk
velvet, silk, beaded fringes. French, 1926-7
Worn by Miss Emilie Grigsby
T.139-1967

1. Obituary, *The Times*, Wednesday 12
February, 1964.

TINY, gleaming,
costume pearls embellish this white satin
bridal corsage by Balmain. It is quilted and beaded all over in a
simple pattern of scallops, each punctuated by a large pearl
flanked by two small pearls. Here, Balmain's handling of
beading is subtle and restrained and makes stylish use of
traditional white satin and pearls.

Closely fitted, the
corsage has a high V-neck, wide shoulders
and set-in, full length sleeves which taper to extremely narrow
wrists, fastening with short zips.

Bridal corsage, satin
embroidered with pearls Pierre Balmain. French, 1946
Given by Stella, Lady Ednam
T.46 & A-1974

JET black sequins and
black glass bugle beads form a densely
patterned surface on this 1961 evening ensemble from Dior.
The black silk ground of the short dress and jacket is entirely
covered by a monochrome pattern created from thousands of
overlapping sequins, which are painstakingly aligned in
different directions to form an diamond trellis design. The
narrow bands that appear to be interwoven are emphasised by
parallel lines of fine bugle beads, over a dense 'ground'
formed in smaller black sequins.

Evening dress and jacket,
'Maxim's', velvet, silk and sequins. Marc Bohan for
Christian Dior. French, Autumn-Winter 1961
Label: Christian Dior
Paris Automne-Hiver 1961 111396
T.130 & A-1974

THIS punk-inspired
dress by Zandra Rhodes is deliberately and decoratively
'ripped' on the bodice and lower skirt, the raw edges of the
slashes emphasised with machine zig-zag stitching in blue
cotton. Beaded gold safety pins and silver ball-link chains are
draped and intertwined in loops which echo the shapes of the
holes, highlighted by a random scattering of bright diamanté.
The fabric, a knitted rayon jersey, clings to the body in a
supple and elastic way, revealing skin through the rents
in a seductive manner.

Evening dress, knitted
rayon jersey, beaded safety pins, ball link
chains, diamanté. Zandra Rhodes. English, London 1977
Label: A Zandra Rhodes Sample
Given by Zandra Rhodes
T.66-1978

THIS 1920's dance dress
is painstakingly embellished with a rich
and vibrant beadwork pattern. The long waisted bodice has a
ground of pale blue cotton muslin which is almost concealed
by a complex, stylised beaded design of pointed stars or
crosses, alternating with long oval cartouches. The cool colour
scheme of white, gold and blue and the tiny, jewel-like glass
beads, set in a timeless design, bring to mind ancient
mosaic or tesserae work.
The simple sleeveless dress has a flared, bias cut skirt, inset
into the waist in zig-zags, which are delineated by gold and
white beads. The deep blue cotton muslin skirt provides a
dramatic background to the clear glass beads
scattered over its surface.

Dance dress, muslin
with beads and sequins. French, c.1925
Given by Mrs J J Arthur Ayres
Circ. 14-1969

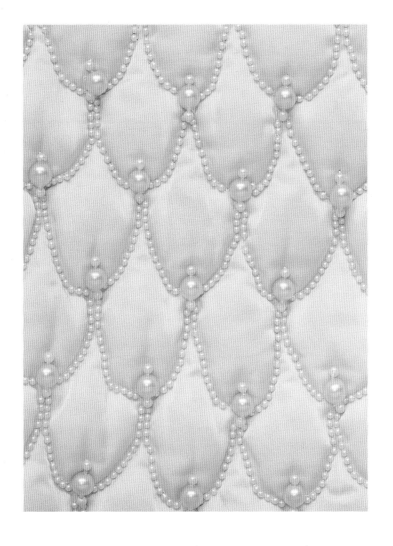

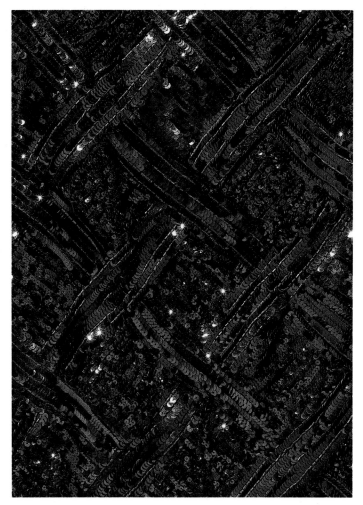

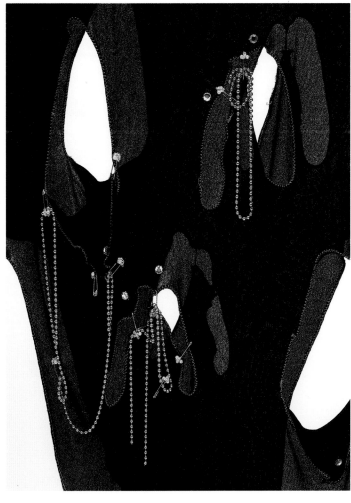

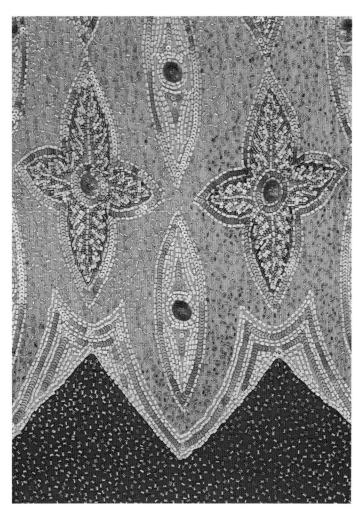

A BRIGHTLY coloured
song bird clinging to a flower stem, is
delicately worked in beads and sequins on this sleeveless tulle
overdress of 1926. Minute blue and turquoise bugle beads form
the bird's body while it's beak and claws are picked out in gold
beads. Iridescent gelatine sequins highlight the raised wing, tail
and breast and its eye is a bright
ruby red bead.

This glistening, frail
garment was worn over a sleeveless satin
dress by the violinist Daisy Kennedy. During recitals light
would catch the beadwork and capture the audience's
attention. Daisy Kennedy was extremely beautiful and a
contemporary portrait of her in this garment shows how it
was held together with a suitably ornate circular
brooch fastened at hip level.

On fragile orange tulle
the open design features flowering
plants picked out with seed pearls and swaying undergrowth in
green, amber and peach beads and sequins. Beaded in a lively
manner the semi-naturalistic design betrays the
influence of Oriental art.

Evening overdress,
tulle, bugle beads, sequins and pearls
Probably French, 1926
Worn by Daisy Kennedy and given by her daughter
Mrs T Moiseiwitsch
T.239-1982

APPLIED DECORATION

GIVENCHY'S dark and
dramatic evening gown is made of
midnight blue silk and spotted black tulle. It has been
embroidered with a repeating pattern of zig-zags in thick,
black silk and flat, metallic thread and scattered with clusters
of bugle and ring beads. Iridescent green-black cockerel
feathers cover the dress and each pendant feather
has been painstakingly attached by its quill. They graduate
from small, soft feathers at the bodice to longer, curved
feathers towards the hem. This serves to
emphasise the gently flaring skirt.

The naturally curving
feathers with their glossy, metallic sheen
create an animated, quivering surface of intense richness.
Feathers have long been used in many different cultures to
adorn and impress humankind. Givenchy harnessed the
decorative and primitive qualities of cockerel plumage for a
sophisticated couture gown with theatrical impact.

Evening gown, silk, tulle, feathers and beads
Hubert de Givenchy. French, Autumn-Winter 1960
Label: Givenchy Paris made in France
Worn and given by Mrs Loel Guinness
T.224-1974

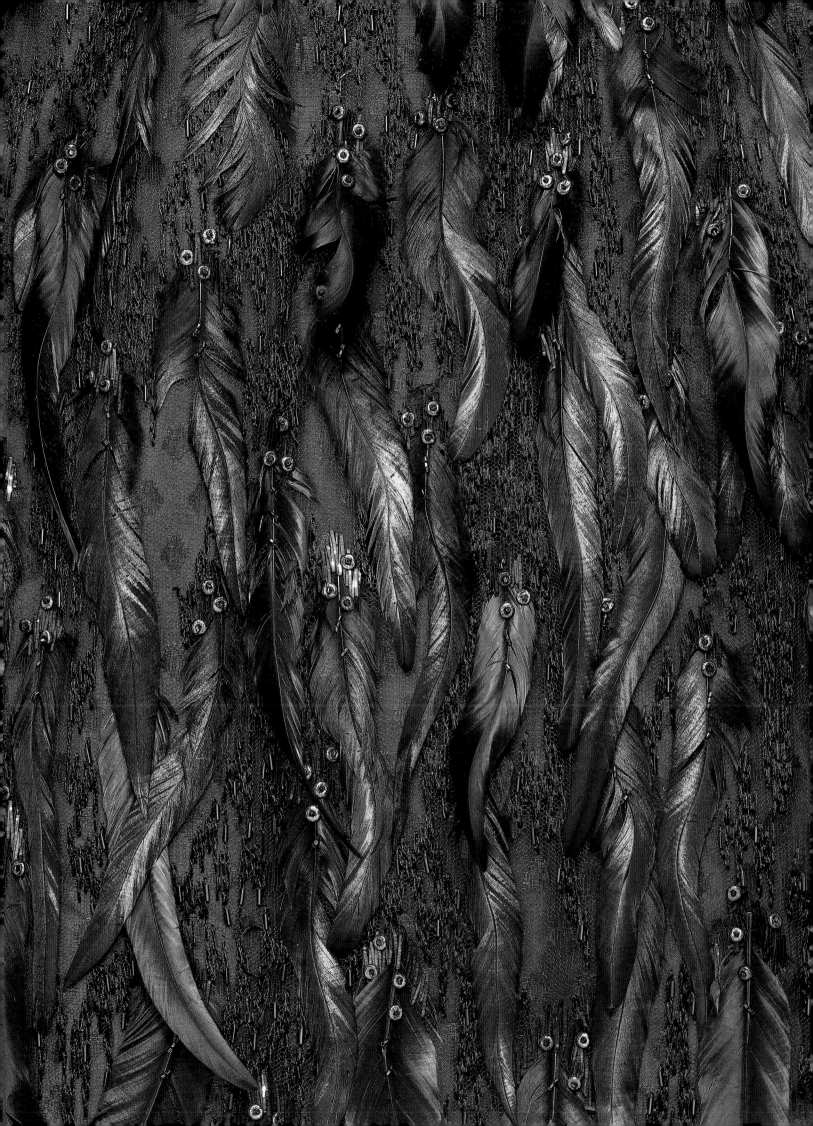

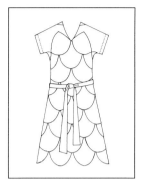 

APPROPRIATELY named 'La
Fleur' is a delicately layered summer
day dress in pale lilac lawn. Its numerous overlapping,
scalloped petals are attached to a tulle base. Each petal encloses
a finely detailed appliquéd motif of a pot containing a
flowering plant. These simple motifs are achieved by a type of
monochromatic shadow work which relies upon the subtle
contrast between opaque and semi-transparent areas. Tiny
pieces of lawn are stitched by hand to the reverse of the fabric
and secured around the edges with minute stitches. Each stitch
draws a few threads together creating lines of small holes.
Similar stitching holds and decorates the gently
waved hem of every petal.

Throughout the
1920s Madeleine Vionnet created couture
collections which revealed her complete mastery of decoration
in dress. As 'La Fleur' illustrates, Vionnet never permitted
pattern to overpower her concepts but used decoration to
achieve impact in a subtle and discreet way.

This meticulously made
dress has the unfitted, tubular shape
that has become synonymous with fashion of the 1920s,
a V-neck, short sleeves and wide sash. It is a *tour de force* in
which an inspired design was executed by highly
skilled needlewomen.

Summer day dress, lawn and tulle with appliqué
Madeleine Vionnet. French, 1920
Worn and given by Sybil, Marchioness
of Cholmondeley
T.444+A-1974

THIS jacket by
Schiaparellli has a resplendent appeal achieved
by the rich juxtaposition of raised embroidery in shining metal
strip tinted lilac and set against dark, imperial purple velvet.
The almost aggressive, large scale floral pattern is worked in
wide metal strip (lama) over thick pads (some of the strips have
moved apart to reveal the padding below). A little of the
original colour has rubbed off and faded to show the
original silver surface of the metal.

The fitted, hip length
jacket is a fairly unremarkable garment
in terms of cut but this serves to concentrate all attention upon
the startling embroidery adorning the wide revers and lower
sleeves. While assessing the immense contribution of Lesage to
French fashion, Palmer White wrote of Schiaparelli: 'No one
couturier has ever done more to promote embroidery than Elsa
Schiaparelli'[1] A further typical Schiaparelli touch is the
button moulded in the shape of a swan, which fastens
the jacket fronts together.

Works by Schiaparelli
illustrate how wholehearted her efforts
were to unite the best of the fine and decorative arts. She
energetically winkled out forgotten skills and craftsmen to
achieve the effects she desired. Breathing new life into these
traditions she was unafraid and used deliberately provocative
combinations of old and new techniques and materials which
she matched with eyecatching designs and arresting
colour combinations.

Evening jacket, silk velvet, purple crepe
Elsa Schiaparelli. French 1938
Worn and given by Madame Schiaparelli
T.51-1965

1. Palmer White, *Haute Couture Embroidery, The Art of Lesage,*
The Vendome Press, 1988

WORN for a wedding
in 1909 this fragile silk chiné gown
appears to have been remodelled from a late 19th century
evening dress. The bride succeeded in combining stylistic ideas
borrowed from 17th century costume with elements that were
highly fashionable in 1909. Wide bands of cream silk Italian
furnishing lace (in the style of early 17th century geometric
Genoese bobbin lace) make the extended bib front and collar.
Three intricate, long tassels hang freely in a graceful line down
the left side of the dress. These elaborate motifs of knotted and
bound twisted ivory silk hanging from fine cords are further
embellished by silk bobbles. This type of decoration was
extremely popular as the *Lady's Realm* commented in 1907
'cords and tassels, after embroideries, take a foremost place in
the world of trimmings'. Fashion periodicals and instruction
manuals informed the less well-off how to make their own
tassels and motifs in silk or cotton. The fine taffeta has a
delicate pastel coloured pattern of floral bouquets and garlands
in soft pinks, blues, greens and yellows and the lace overlay
allows enticing glimpses of the silk chiné beneath. The
attractively blurred pattern was achieved by
dyeing the warp threads before weaving.

The unpicking and
re-making of clothes is part of the history
of fashionable dress and for this wedding dress juxtaposition
of late 19th century and early 20th century materials and
trimmings has been accomplished with skill. The full length
gown has a low décolletage and wide, elbow length sleeves
with narrow frills of taffeta at the cuffs below which deep,
hanging cuffs of late 19th century revival lace appear. In
keeping with the 1908-9 fashion for a slightly raised waist the
full skirt is gathered into a high waistline and encircled by a
draped sash which is secured at the back with two bow
tabs fastened by Art Nouveau buttons.

Rustling silk patterned with pretty pastel coloured flowers, a
romantic style inspired by historical dress and feminine tassels
and lace (albeit furnishing lace) unite in this delicately
attractive wedding gown.

Wedding gown, chiné
silk taffeta, revival lace and tassels. English, 1909
Worn by Mrs P Adams at her wedding in 1909
Given by the friends of the late Pearl Adams
T.52-1957

THIS summer day dress
in matt crepe of the palest blue-green is
an outstanding example of Madeleine Vionnet's art. Intricate,
meticulously executed drawn threadwork adorns the bodice
front, bodice back and sleeves and takes its diamond shaped
grid from the lie of the warp and weft in the bias-cut fabric. A
zig-zag openwork seam joins yoke and bodice and provides
more flexibility and suppleness than a conventional seam.
Vionnet's innovative bias cutting techniques permitted the
matt silk crepe (woven to her specifications) to follow the
contours of the body.

Afternoon dress,
matt silk crepe. Madeleine Vionnet. French 1932-4
Worn by Lady Dovercourt and
given in her name by Mrs Amy Bird
T.197&A-1973

A COMPLEX, abstract
pattern in soutache is applied over the
jacket of this top quality day ensemble (the original design is
named 'Sybille') of 1907 by Paquin. Plain, woollen eau-de-nil
facecloth forms the matt background for the gleaming braid
which is stitched down in a design of large curved motifs and
diagonal lines over bodice and sleeves. The narrow braid was
handled with great precision by skilled seamstresses in the
embroidery workshop and the design achieves a satisfactory
balance between plain and decorated areas.

Walking costume, jacket and
skirt, woollen facecloth and soutache braid 'Sybille'
Madame Paquin. French, Summer 1907
Worn by Mrs Henry Paul Carrington
Given by Miss H Carrington
T.73 to C-1967

PIERRE Cardin is famous
for the futuristic clothes he designed
in the 1960s many of which were displayed in the 1990
retrospective exhibition of his haute couture [1]. Less overtly
space age is this mini-dress in powder blue crepe with clean,
sharp lines echoed in the linear decoration around the flared
hem. The quilted geometric pattern is the only embellishment
on this otherwise plain dress. Pierre Cardin insists that a
design should never be overloaded with ideas and that one
strong decorative feature is sufficient.

Mini-dress, crepe
Pierre Cardin. French, 1967-8
Worn and given by Mrs A Wallrock T.260-1983

1. *Pierre Cardin,
Past, Present, Future*, V&A, 1990-1

TWO enormous fronds
embroidered in cream silk chenille
sweep across the rustling black taffeta skirt of a *robe de style*
designed by Jeanne Lanvin for winter 1922-3. Chenille (the
French for caterpillar) is a round furry yarn resembling its living
namesake. Here its soft, velvety pile is set against a crisp paper taffeta.
The dress has an
immaculately piped boat neckline and flared,
capped sleeves and its long, floating skirt is minutely gathered
into the natural waistline. Luxurious but restrained, the
chenille fronds curve from waist to just above the hem and
draw attention to the bell-like, spreading skirt.

Robe de style, silk
taffeta with georgette and chenille
Jeanne Lanvin. French, winter 1922-3
Label: Jeanne Lanvin Paris Unis- France
T.334-1978

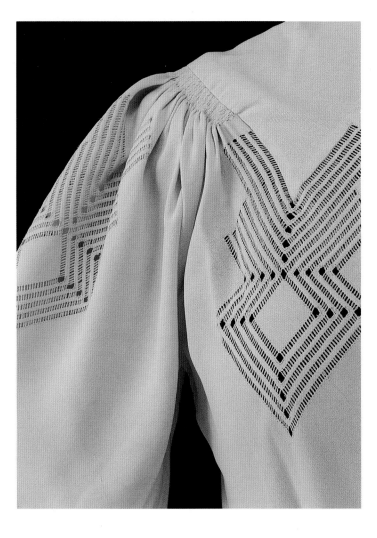

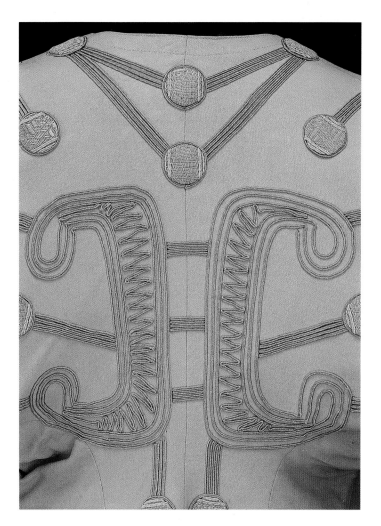

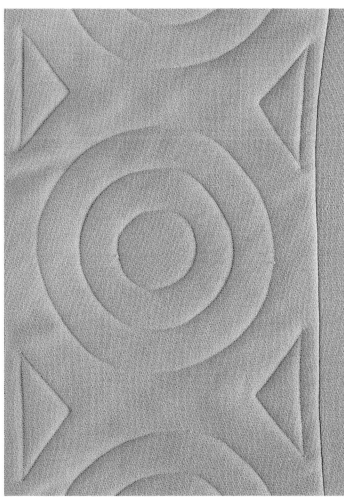

MACHINE embroidered
daisies are repeated in a neat, precise
pattern over this summer mini-dress designed by André
Courrèges. The bold, padded flowers stand proud of the
surface and their scalloped petals are worked in satin stitched
white cotton beneath pink organza overlays with oversewn
edges. The flower centres are glimmering discs of iridescent
perspex and in technique, resemble Indian mirror-work
embroidery known as *abhla bharat*. This sleeveless, flared
mini-dress of transluscent, white, rippled nylon organza has an
evanescent quality which is given substance by the bold
pattern. Raised, machine embroidered bands encircle and
emphasise the neck, armholes,
hem and waist.

A-line mini-dresses
designed by Courrèges achieved a little girl
look with their high waisted bodices and short flared skirts and
became enormously influential in the 1960s. In this particular
example Courrèges combined nylon, plastic and innovatory
Swiss embroidery to produce a celebration of all that was
considered modern in 1967. He completed this fresh, young,
up-to-date style with white kid boots, cropped white gloves
and futuristic, white plastic sunglasses.

Mini-dress, nylon organza and cotton
André Courrèges. French 1967. Label: Courrèges Paris
Given by Mrs G Sacher
T.348-1975

STUDWORK embellishes
the entire surface of this black leather
jacket from Katherine Hamnett's winter 1990 'Clean Up or
Die' collection. Hexagonal facetted studs and round studs are
firmly rivetted through the leather to create blocks of pattern
broken by short, heavy zips. The origin of metal studwork
is somewhat obscure although since the 1950s, the black
leather biking jacket has been adopted by disaffected youth
as a symbol of rebellion and defiance. 'Every
revolt needs a uniform'[1]

A black leather jacket
'the clothing of pure affront'[2] is
associated with teenage menace as well as the glamour
embodied by Marlon Brando in the film *The Wild One* (1954).
Hard metal studs could offer additional surface armour on an
already highly protective and sturdy garment but Katherine
Hamnett's stud designs are less aggressive; high fashion
reworkings of tough street wear. Beneath the forceful leathers
the man wears a classic Hamnett slogan T-shirt and trousers
whereas his female counterpart sports a
slinky, velour catsuit.

Wittily, Katherine
Hamnett autographs one jacket with her
initials set into a heart shape. The jacket back is emblazoned,
not with nihilistic Hell's Angels' mottoes, but with the
environmental plea 'Clean up or Die'.

Jacket, leather and metal studwork
Katherine Hamnett. English, winter 1990
Given by Katherine Hamnett
T.208-1990

1. Mick Farren, *The
Black Leather Jacket*, Abbeville Press, 1985
2. Angela Carter, 'Notes For a Theory of Sixties Style',
New Society, 14 December 1967

THE shocking pink,
silk faille ground of this evening coat by
Balenciaga is almost obliterated by an abstract pattern of
transluscent, pink plastic discs enclosed by pink chenille zig-
zag overstitching, glass beads, pink rhinestones and silver and
pink embroidered metal threads. Weighty silk faille and lavish
embroidery make the garment extremely heavy. Balenciaga is
famous for his uncompromisingly austere designs. Perhaps less
well known is his more flamboyant side exemplified by this
lavish coat. Custom made for Balenciaga this adventurous
embroidery incorporates modern materials and celebrates
one of his favourite 'Spanish' colours.

Balenciaga made
buttonholes in the most difficult materials
and was not even deterred by heavily embroidered fabrics.
Nestling in the centre of the detail is a tiny button covered in
silk faille and embroidered to match
the evening coat.

The three quarter
length coat has a simple round neck and
elbow length sleeves while darts at the back and front shape it
tightly into the waist. It was originally worn with a straight,
dark skirt, long gloves and a feathered,
side-swept hat.

Evening coat, silk faille
embroidered with plastic, rhinestones, beads and gilt threads
Cristobal Balenciaga. Embroidery, Lesage
French, August 1961
Label: Balenciaga 10 Avenue George V Paris
Worn and given by Mrs Loel Guinness
T.24-1974

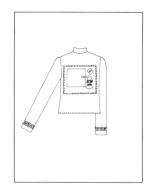

LUN-NA Menoh is a
fashion designer whose clothes often
resemble pieces of sculpture and she always incorporates a
story into each of her works. The detail shows part of the
layered net overdress where appliqué is used to create the
forest in her fairy-tale narrative. In an amusing, *faux naïf* way
the wood is suggested by applied strips of felt with pinked
edges topstitched in white cotton and overlapping lengths
of green, blue and white rick-rack. Additional braid and
yellow ribbon inscribed with instructions are
visible through the net haze.

This particular ensemble
complete with hat, shoes, violin case
and wearing instructions was conceived as a quest and the
wearer must follow signs variously applied to the outfit in the
hope of finding the missing musical instrument. As Lun-na
Menoh's instructions are self-denying, the instrument can
never be found and the wearer is 'snared in a
circular path without escape'.

A short, sleeveless,
net overtunic with fur trimmed neck and
widely flared hem (wired to project like a crinoline) is worn
over a green velvet top (complete with panel of instructions
and a pixie in relief) and matching knee length,
shirred velvet pants.

The simple, direct and versatile technique of appliqué is
employed to create a whimsical, off-beat outfit.

Ensemble 'Looking for
a musical instrument – wearing a paradox',
velvet, net and fur
Lun-na Menoh (Atsuko Shimizu). Japan 1989
T.272 to G-1989

MARY Quant's red
seersucker mini-dress uses bright,
inexpensive materials for maximum impact and takes
inspiration from traditional English country smocks and
children's pinafores of the late 19th century. The pin-tucked
bodice front and back are trimmed with double rows of shiny
green soutache braid, which are tied in loose bows with their
raw ends knotted to prevent fraying. Green rick-rack braid
edges the square neck, circular oversleeves, hemline and centre
back which is fastened with large
red plastic buttons.

Mini dress, cotton seersucker, braid trimming
Mary Quant. English 1972
Label: Mary Quant Made in Great Britain
Given by Mary Quant
T.113-1976

PAUL Poiret's renowned
use of opulent colour is displayed to
the full in this emerald green, purple and gold opera cloak of
about 1912. The main part of the ankle length garment is cut
from a single piece of finely ribbed silk which is turned back at
the centre front to create deep revers. Weighted by an
enormously heavy, deep gilt fringe of metallic sprung coils (as
used in dress uniforms), the hem dips steeply down to side
points. Gold is used again to great effect in the large and
elaborate frogged loop and button which fastens the cloak at
hip level. The ingenious gold and gun metal grey button is
constructed in concentric circles of rouleaux.

Opera cloak, ribbed silk,
figured silk and metal threads. Paul Poiret. French c.1912
Label: Paul Poiret à Paris Given by Lady Gladwyn and
worn by her mother Lady Noble
T.337-1974

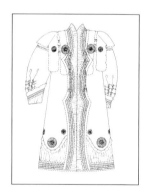

A SUMMER evening
wrap in eau-de-nil silk taffeta is ornately
decorated with sunflowers which were among the most
popular motifs in late 19th and early 20th century applied arts.
These extraordinarily large sunflowers (diameter 14 cms) are
applied around the hem above a lace edged, deep and scalloped
border of ruched silk. Steeply pointed, the sunflower's white
cotton petals are overlapped around centres of tightly ruched
taffeta. This rich growth is concentrated around the hem
although a few sunflowers adorn the bodice and smaller
versions bloom on the shoulders.

Evening wrap,
silk taffeta. Probably French, 1904
Worn by Lady Fairhaven and given by Major
and Mrs Broughton
T.273-1972

FOR wearing on winter
evenings, a dark rose pink velvet cloak
by Liberty is trimmed at the hem with appliqué motifs above a
deep fur band. In gold satin, the applied shapes are deeply
padded (in the manner of theatrical costume) to create a
pattern of ovals and dimpled circles within double rows of
embroidered gilt threads. Picking up the gold theme, two gilt
tassels hang from shaped flaps at the lower back. The deep hem
of soft brown marabou fur, completes the warm cloak and, in
matching fur, a high collar fastens snugly around the
neck with a single button.

Evening cloak, velvet, marabou fur and satin
Liberty & Co. English, c.1920
Label: Liberty & Co. London and Paris
Worn and given by Mrs R Craggs
T.238-1963

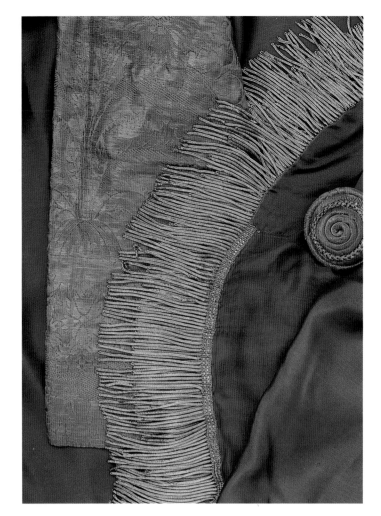

SIMPLICITY and grace
are the key notes of this floor length,
white chiffon evening robe of about 1936. With the Jeanne
Lanvin hallmark of understated elegance, the frail semi-
transparent fabric is inventively decorated with machine
stitched, appliqué strips of gilded kid leather. Each minute
strip is precisely positioned and carefully stitched around the
edges to form a strong and regular vertical pattern over the
entire garment. Like a shower of gold the shining strips appear
to fall continuously and emphasise the gown's flowing style. It
has an unfitted bodice and voluminous bishop sleeves which
are gathered into the wrists. A columar skirt falls from the
gathered waist in soft folds to the
leather trimmed hem.

A totally refined yet
opulent colour scheme of gold on white creates a subtle
garment with virginal overtones.

Evening gown,
silk chiffon and gilded kid leather
Jeanne Lanvin. French, c.1936
Given by Lady Glenconner
T.61-1967

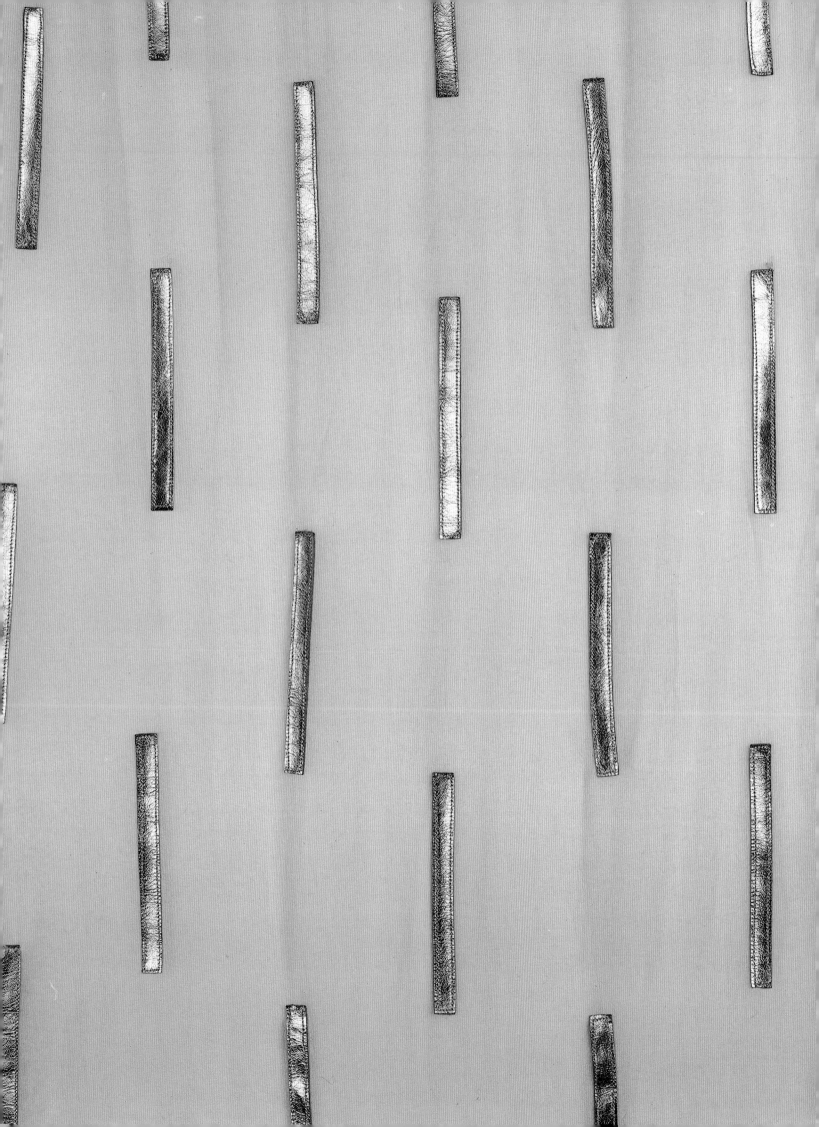

Appliqué A method of
applying decoration to the surface of a fabric usually
by stitching pieces of other fabrics or
trimmings on to it.

Chenille A furry thread
like a caterpillar – hence the name.
A fabric is woven with the warp threads in groups. It is then
cut along the length between the groups. The thread thus
formed is used in both woven textiles and embroidery.

Chiné A method of
printing warp threads before weaving.
The weft is not printed so the pattern has a misty appearance
when woven.

Crepe Usually a dress
weight fabric with a textured surface
achieved in various ways; use of hard-twisted yarns, the
application of heat or chemicals, or by
a special crepe weave.

Damask weave A single
colour, reversible fabric in which the
pattern is formed by contrast of shiny warp face areas and
matt weft face areas.

Dolman sleeve A sleeve
that is cut in one piece with the
bodice and thus has no seam around the arm socket. It is wide
and creates a deep armhole which almost
reaches the waist.

Face cloth A high
quality, medium-weight wool with a slightly raised, lustrous,
dense surface.

Fagotting 1) Decorative
insertion stitches used to join two
pieces of hemmed fabric together. 2) A type of
drawn threadwork.

Foulard A soft twill
weave silk, plain or printed, much used
for making scarves. The French for
'scarf' is *un foulard*.

Frogging Braid or cord
made into decorative patterns around
looped fastenings. Once used on
military uniforms.

Gabardine A tightly woven twill weave fabric.

Godet A triangular or
gathered or pleated section of material
inserted (usually at the hem) to give a garment fullness
and assist movement.

Grosgrain A term for a heavily ribbed silk.

Gusset A small, triangular or diamond-shaped piece of
material inserted under the arms or crotch to aid movement
and facilitate the garment's fit.

Leg of Mutton sleeves
They were cut narrow on the forearm
and wider at the upper arm so that when gathered into the
shoulder they resembled a leg of mutton or 'gigot'.

Picot A decorative
edge to a hem often made by cutting
through pre-worked fagotting or machine
hem-stitching.

Pinking Serrated finishing
for a raw edge trimmed using a pair
of notched 'pinking shears' for decorative effect or to
stop it from fraying.

Raglan sleeve Cut so
that a diagonal seam runs across the
front and back of the garment from the underarm to a point at
the neck line. The sleeve itself is often
cut in two sections.

Rayon Name adopted
to replace 'artificial silk'. Generic term
for filaments made from modified cellulose. It was the first
man-made fibre to be mass-produced. Developed in the late
19th century, it became more widely available from
the First World War.

Robe de style French term
for a dress with a tight fitting
bodice and a bouffant, full skirt, sleeveless or
with short sleeves.

Rouleau A narrow
tube of fabric (usually cut on the cross)
turned so that the raw edges are inside. Cord or padding is
sometimes inserted to stiffen the tube. Often used for
decoration or to make fastenings and sometimes
to neaten an edge.

Satin A warp faced
weave which gives a smooth and shiny
surface. Usually used for silk or
man-made fibres.

Selvedge The finished
edges running along the length of a
piece of woven cloth.

GLOSSARY

Shirring Several rows
of gathers. Can be used decoratively by
itself or can have embroidery or smocking
sewn over it.

Topstitching A line or
lines of stitching sewn from the right
side, or top, of a fabric. Usually
used decoratively.

Tussah silk A wild silk.

Twill A way of
weaving cloth which produces a diagonal rib
across the cloth.

Welt An extra strip of material stitched to an edge or seam.

Whitework Embroidery
worked with white thread on a white
ground.

Adburgham, Alison,
Shops and Shopping 1800-1914, George
Allen & Unwin, 1964.

Arnold, Janet,
Patterns of Fashion 2 c 1860-1940,
Macmillan 1977.

Barthes, Roland,
The Fashion System, Jonathan Cape, 1985.

Beaton, Cecil,
The Glass of Fashion, Weidenfeld
& Nicolson, 1954.

Bernard, Barbara,
Fashion in the 1960s, Academy
Editions, 1978

Coleman, E A,
The Genius of Charles James Holt Rinehart &
Winston for the Brooklyn
Museum, 1982

Deslandres, Yvonne
& Müller, Florence, *Histoire de la Mode
au XXe siècle,* Somogy,
Paris, 1974.

Deslandres, Yvonne,
Paul Poiret, Thames & Hudson, 1987.

Ewing, Elizabeth,
History of Twentieth Century Fashion,
Batsford, 1974.

Giroud, Francoise, *Dior,* Thames & Hudson, 1987.

Hardingham, Martin,
The Illustrated Dictionary of Fabrics,
Studio Vista, 1978.

Johnston, Lorraine (ed)
The Fashion Year, Zomba Books, 1985.

Jouve, Marie-Andrée,
Balenciaga, Editions du Regard,
Paris, 1988.

Keenan, Brigid,
Dior in Vogue, Octopus Books, 1981.

Lee, Sarah Tomerlin, *American Fashion,*
André Deutsch, 1975.

Leeds City Art Galleries, *Jean Muir,* 1980.

London, Geffrye Museum,
*Utility Fashion and Furniture
1941-1951,* 1974.

London, V&A,
Fashion An anthology by Cecil Beaton,
HMSO, 1971.

London, V&A, *Ascher, Fabric Art Fashion,* 1987.

Lurie, Alison,
The Language of Clothes, Heinemann, 1982.

Lynam, Ruth, (ed) *Paris Fashion,* Michael Joseph, 1972.

Lyon, Musée
Historique des Tissus, *Mariano
Fortuny Venise,* 1980.

Lyon, Musée
Historique des Tissus, *Hommage à
Balenciaga,* 1985.

McDowell, Colin,
*McDowell's Directory of Twentieth Century
Fashion,* Frederick Muller, 1984.

Mansfield, Alan &
Cunnington, Phillis, *Handbook of Costume
in the 20th century 1900-1950,*
Faber & Faber, 1973.

Marly, Diana de,
The History of Couture 1850-1950,
Batsford, 1980.

Mendes, Valerie,
Pierre Cardin: Past Present Future, Dirk
Nishen, 1990.

Millbank, Caroline, *Couture,* Thames & Hudson, 1985.

Mulvagh, Jane,
Vogue History of 20th Century Fashion,
Viking, 1988.

New York,
The Metropolitan Museum, *Yves Saint Laurent*, 1983.

Osma, Guillermo
de, *Fortuny, His Life and His Work*,
Aurum Press, 1980.

Paris, Musée de la
Mode et du Costume, Palais Galliera,
*Pierre Balmain, 40 Années de
Création*, 1985.

Paris, Musée de
la Mode, *Hommage à Christian Dior
1947-1957*, 1986.

Polan, Brenda (ed),
The Fashion Year, Zomba Books, 1983.

Polan, Brenda (ed),
The Fashion Year, Zomba Books, 1984.

Rhodes, Zandra &
Knight, Anne, *The Art of Zandra Rhodes*,
Jonathan Cape, 1984.

Robinson, Julian,
Fashion in the 30s, Oresko
Books, 1978.

Rothstein, Natalie (ed),
400 Years of Fashion, V&A and
Collins, 1984.

White, Palmer,
Elsa Schiaparelli, Aurum Press, 1986.

Wilson, Elizabeth,
Adorned in Dreams: Fashion and Modernity,
Virago, 1985.

York, Peter, *Style Wars*, Sidgwick
& Jackson, 1978.

SELECTED READING LIST

Unless otherwise stated the books are published in London.